Over fifty years have passed since the first volume of the Penguin *Famous Trials* appeared. This re-issue of nine volumes of the famous series covering notorious crimes and trials from the mid nineteenth century onwards remains true to the original text and just as fascinating to modern readers.

The Penguin *Famous Trials* series has its origins in *The Notable British Trials Series* which was founded in 1905 by Harry Hodge. As Managing Director of William Hodge & Co. Ltd, Publishers and Shorthand Writers, Hodge had a vast knowledge of both the Scottish Courts and criminology – he was himself an expert shorthand writer and this is reflected in his careful selection of editors and his insistence on accurate reporting of trials for *The Notable British Trials Series*. As the original editor of the Penguin *Famous Trials* (Volumes 1 and 2), Hodge chose the most intriguing crimes, remaining firm to his belief that a crime should be at least twenty years old before it can prove itself 'notable'. After his death in 1947 his son, James Hozier Hodge, went on to become general editor of the Penguin *Famous Trials* series.

FAMOUS TRIALS 6

Thurtell and Hunt
Frederick Nodder
Peter Barnes and others
John George Haigh

EDITED BY JAMES H. HODGE

PENGUIN BOOKS

PENGUIN BOOKS

Published by the Penguin Group
Penguin Books Ltd, 27 Wrights Lane, London W8 5TZ, England
Penguin Books USA Inc., 375 Hudson Street, New York, New York 10014, USA
Penguin Books Australia Ltd, Ringwood, Victoria, Australia
Penguin Books Canada Ltd, 10 Alcorn Avenue, Toronto, Ontario, Canada M4V 3B2
Penguin Books (NZ) Ltd, 182–190 Wairau Road, Auckland 10, New Zealand

Penguin Books Ltd, Registered Offices: Harmondsworth, Middlesex, England

First published in the Notable British Trials Series by
William Hodge & Co. Ltd
(*Thurtell and Hunt*, 1951; Frederick Nodder, 1950; Peter Barnes
and others, 1953; John George Haigh, 1953)
These abridged versions published in Penguin Books 1962
3 5 7 9 10 8 6 4 2

Copyright © William Hodge & Company (Holdings) Ltd, 1962
All rights reserved

Printed in England by Clays Ltd, St Ives plc

Contents

Preface

THE four trials selected for this sixth volume in the Penguin *Famous Trials* series have, as before, been taken from the *Notable British Trials* series, where the reader can find in each individual volume the full evidence in the case in question and a considerable amount of additional material. Thurtell and Hunt, who engendered tremendous press space and voluminous broadsheet publications in the early nineteenth century, present a picture of swindlers, gamblers, phoney boxing matches, and the behaviour of the followers of the turf in bygone days. In more modern vein there is the unpleasant figure of Frederick Nodder, who stood two trials for the abduction and murder of a child, and who was responsible for a police search of mammoth proportions. His first trial is notable for the many passages at arms between the unique Mr Justice Swift and the patient counsel appearing before him in Court. The trial of Peter Barnes and others is a good example of the troubles caused in England in 1939 by the Irish Republican Army which have tended to be obscured by the Second World War. This was murder directed indiscriminately by a terrorist against the community by means of a bomb left in the heart of Coventry. Haigh, as a mass murderer for gain, whose confidence and vanity make him unique of his kind, still holds his lofty position in this class of crime alongside Peter Manuel and Reg Christie who were to follow. Altogether they make an interesting cross-section of occupants of the dock, and it is to be hoped that the lesser known events will provide interest for the reader; it is not always the Madeleine Smiths, the Crippens, or the Seddons who provide the best fare, although by constant repetition they may continue to be household names in the realm of infamy.

Had the Homicide Act of 1957 been in force when these trials took place, different results might have been forthcoming in several of them. The rather curious classification of capital murder, and the introduction of diminished responsibility as a means of reducing a murder charge to that of manslaughter (already in force in Scotland for some years under the heading of culpable homicide), would certainly have changed the ending of at least one of these cases. Nodder, as revolting a character as any criminal, could not have been hanged. He did not commit a crime in the furtherance of theft, nor did he use a gun; and he only carried out one murder. Therefore in his case he could only have been tried for non-capital murder, despite the fact that he abducted, despoiled, and killed a little girl of ten. Had he shot her, he would have hanged. Surely this is a curious situation. Peter Barnes, on the other hand, would most likely have been hanged for his part in the Coventry explosion, although in his own way he was a decent young man whose main fault was a misguided sense of patriotism in which he merely acted the part of carrier of the explosive material used in the outrage. Both Thurtell and Hunt would have come under a hanging sentence, for they certainly acted with a theft motive and used a pistol to carry out their purpose. Indeed, Hunt could not nowadays have been transported, and would likely have followed Thurtell to the gallows. It is possible that Haigh might have got away with diminished responsibility, through mental unsoundness bordering on, although not amounting to, insanity, whereby he could only partially have been held responsible for his actions, but in view of his very able handling of his victims' affairs after death, and the fact that he gained financially all the time, especially when he was embarrassed for cash, it is unlikely that he would have been successful in his pleadings, though at least the jury would have been invited to study the case from that point of view. It is hardly surprising that the law of murder today perplexes many with its apparent inconsistencies.

J. H. H.

Thurtell and Hunt

· 1824 ·

BY

E. R. WATSON

At Hertford Winter Assizes on 6 January 1824, before Mr Justice Park and a jury, John Thurtell was charged with the murder of William Weare. Alongside him in the dock stood two of his cronies, Joseph Hunt and William Probert, charged as accessories before the fact. No evidence was offered against Probert, who was formally acquitted and gave vital evidence against the other two men. The trial ended on the second day with the conviction of both the accused. Thurtell was hanged on 9 January, the time lag being negligible as was the custom of those days, and on 16 March Hunt was transported. It is interesting to note that in June 1825 Probert was hanged for horse-stealing – a relatively trivial affair compared with the part he took in Weare's murder.

The murder, although extremely callous and brutal, was not of itself particularly noteworthy, but the circumstances in which the main characters lived and the immense publicity of the case place it as one of the foremost events in the criminal calendar of last century. It was nearly the last case to take place under the old Tudor procedure, which was almost an inquisition, and it was the first 'trial by newspaper'. During the hearing there was a serious collision between the Bench and the Press as to the duties of the latter in relation to the detection of crime and its investigation.

All four of the principal characters were men who lived by their wits in some form or another. Thurtell, who came from respected stock, devoted most of his time to the professional boxing ring and was mixed up in rigged fights, continuous gambling, and fraud. Hunt was the manager of a tavern where he met Thurtell, and had already been in trouble. Probert was a bankrupt wine-merchant of a very shifty nature and at the time of the murder had a lease of Gill's Hill Cottage, near Elstree in Hertfordshire. He was under notice to leave on account of not paying his rent. Weare, the ex-waiter, who was killed near the cottage, was a billiard player and sharper who frequented gambling dens. He was reputed always to carry substantial sums of money on him, and at the time in question was supposed to owe Thurtell some cash. He had recently returned from Doncaster races. The motive of his murder through the conspiracy of the other three was entirely one of gain.

On Friday, 24 October 1823, Weare left his lodgings at Lyon's Inn in a hackney coach, complete with a double-barrelled gun, backgammon board and dice, and a green carpet bag. He was driven to the New Road, where he paid off his coach and got into a gig with John Thurtell, who as far as he knew was to drive him down to Gill's Hill Cottage for a few days' stay. In point of fact, the cottage was very small and already overcrowded, but in any case it was never intended that he should get there alive. The gig was observed on various stages of its route to the cottage, and just after 8 p.m. that evening two people saw it being driven past Probert's house at a great pace with two men in it answering the description of Thurtell and Weare. Five minutes later some other person heard the sound of a shot about 400 yards away, followed by the voices of two men in angry argument, succeeded by groans which deepened until they died away. The spot from which the groans came was a quarter of a mile from Probert's cottage.

On this same Friday morning two men, answering in every respect to the description of Thurtell and Hunt, purchased a pair of pistols from a pawnbroker in Marylebone. In the middle of the day Hunt hired a gig at one place and a horse at another, under pretension of going to Dartford in Kent. He inquired where he could procure a sack and a rope, and these he obtained at some other place nearby. Thurtell, Hunt, and Probert, together with Thurtell's brother and a man named Noyes who had nothing to do with the murder, assembled at the Coach and Horses in Conduit Street the same afternoon. Having prepared all that was wanted in the gig, Hunt told Thurtell that everything was ready. Thurtell drove off from the house alone between four and five, having previously requested Probert to bring Hunt down with him in his own gig as he (Thurtell) was to take up a friend 'to be killed as he travelled with him', an expression which Probert said he believed at the time to be a piece of idle bravado. From Conduit Street Thurtell drove to pick up his companion at the New Road.

After Thurtell's departure, Hunt and Probert left the Coach and Horses in the latter's gig and, having a better horse, overtook Weare and Thurtell on the road. They stopped at several public houses, and at one of these stopping places the other two passed them in turn, unperceived. Tired of waiting, Hunt and Probert then went on until they reached a place called Phillimore Lodge, about a mile beyond Edgware, where Hunt got out of the gig saying that he had been told to do so by Thurtell. Probert drove on, and met Thurtell on foot in a lane near Gill's Hill Cottage. Having asked where Hunt was, Thurtell said he had done it without his assistance, for he had killed 'that Weare'. Probert went back for Hunt who told him that the murder was supposed to have been carried out where he had left the gig and that the intention had been do to it with his assistance. Hunt was then driven back towards the cottage, and when Thurtell reproached him for not being punctual he said that it was of no consequence because Thurtell had the tools. Thurtell replied that the pistols were little better than popguns, for he had fired them in his companion's face without success as the bullets had glanced off. Weare had got out of the chaise and run away, crying out that he would give Thurtell back his money if he would spare his life. Thurtell had then followed him and cut his throat; even this had not been enough, for he ran the pistol into his skull, turned it through his brains, and killed him.

The three men went into the cottage where Probert introduced his companions to his wife and a Miss Noyes, after which arrangements were made for supper. Obviously no visitors had been expected, for in addition to the two women the maid and Probert's children were also in the house. The men left the cottage, ostensibly to call on a neighbour, but in fact to go to the spot where the murder had been committed. Thurtell dragged the body, which had been enveloped in a sack from head to knees, through a hedge into the lane, and then rifled the pockets, saying he had in the first instance taken a fourth part of the property. On returning to the cottage Thurtell went to the stable and sponged himself with care in order to wipe off the bloodstains, many of which were seen by Probert's stable boy.

After supper Thurtell produced a gold watch chain which he presented to Mrs Probert; it was suitable for either a man's or a woman's watch. He and Hunt arranged to sit up for the night on account of the lack of accommodation. Late at night the three men went down to the lane again to remove the body, but because of its weight they had to throw it across one of the horses. It was brought to the garden of the cottage and then dragged across to a pond, stones were put in the sack, and the body thrown into the water. From an upstairs window Mrs Probert saw something being dragged across the garden, which she supposed to be a corpse. Her suspicion aroused, she went downstairs and listened at the parlour door. The men divided the contents of Weare's purse and pocket-book, allotting to each man his share amounting to five or six pounds.

In the morning, Hunt and Thurtell were in the lane as early as six o'clock. They found a man working there, and as he was searching about for something in the hedge they said they had nearly been capsized in the gig the night before. After they left, the man, who was not satisfied, examined the spot and found traces of blood, a bloody knife, and a pocket pistol with marks of blood and human brains on it.

Probert was determined that the body of Weare should not remain in his pond, as he well knew he would be charged with murder should it be found. Accordingly Thurtell and Hunt agreed to move it on the following Monday. They drove back to London in two gigs, taking with them Probert's stable boy as a precaution, finally leaving him at the Coach and Horses. According to agreement the two men returned to Gill's Hill Cottage at 10 p.m. on the Monday night, and while Hunt kept the women in conversation, Probert and Thurtell drew the body from the pond. It was then put in Thurtell's gig, and he and Hunt drove to a brook on the north side of Elstree where it was sunk in the same way as on the previous Friday. The bottom of the gig was covered in mud and blood.

Rumours were rife in the vicinity of the crime because of the report of the pistol or gun shot that had been heard in the lane. These rumours came to the ears of the magistrates, and a search was made near the spot. In consequence of certain communications, Thurtell, Hunt, and Probert were apprehended, and shortly afterwards, on 30 October, the body was found.

*

John Thurtell, like many another graceless scamp, was the son of well-to-do, pre-eminently respectable, God-fearing parents of the middle class. He was born on 21 December 1794, one of a large family whose head, John Thurtell senior, was a prosperous Norwich merchant who lived near Harford Bridge, two miles southward of that provincial capital.

He seems to have been the eldest son, and was, as the worst behaved child generally is, the favourite of his mother. He did not apparently leave home to go to a boarding school, and may have received the rudiments of education at the Norwich Grammar School. Wherever he studied he did so to little purpose, for at the age of thirty he was capable of writing, 'I feel greatly oblidge.' He does not seem to have displayed the early depravity of a Cartouche, and his friend George Borrow, the famous author, has preserved no worse instance of his evil tendencies at this period than the tying of a canister to a dog's tail (*The Romany Rye*, Chapter 42). Throughout life he was choleric, vindictive, generally silent in company, and with no conversation beyond bawdy and blasphemy, the 'fancy', and the stage. His constitution was robust, his animal spirits high, and among his cronies he often showed great good humour and was always free with his money.

Such being his disposition, an active career was determined for him, and on 8 May 1809 he received his commission as second lieutenant in Company 99 of Marines, whose headquarters were at Chatham. He proceeded thither, and spent a very brief period learning his duties on shore. There was then lying in the Medway, refitting, H.M.S. *Adamant*, fifty guns, carrying the flag of Rear-Admiral Sir Edmund Nagle, commanded by Captain John Sykes. Thurtell was added to her strength on 4 June 1809. After some uneventful cruises in home waters – in the Downs, off the Nore, and as far as the mouth of the Zuyder Zee – the vessel was ordered to North Britain as the Admiral's flagship in those parts, and for several years she lay moored in Leith Roads, with very occasional trips to sea. For a year after her arrival in the roads Thurtell remained one of her company, with no scope for honourable ambitions or for that display of courage in the face of death which lent his last moments a trace of unwonted, if theatrical, dignity. The lure of a great city, it may be, drew him, as often as he could get leave, to seek a questionable excitement among its least reputable haunts. At the end of August 1810, Sir Edmund Nagle hauled down his flag, and was succeeded by Rear-Admiral William Otway, Mathew Buckle at the same time replacing Sykes in the command of the ship.

On 16 July 1811, John Thurtell, for some slight misdemeanour the nature of which does not appear, was peremptorily discharged 'by the personal order of Rear-Admiral Otway', his place being taken by John Alexander, who came aboard in the *Eliza* tender.

Thurtell's next ship was the *Bellona*, seventy-four guns, commanded by Captain J. E. Douglas and later by Captain George Mackinlay, on whose muster-roll he remained from 7 November 1811, having been conveyed to that vessel, then at sea, by the *Theseus*, seventy-four guns, to which he had been transferred from the *Monmouth*. For several months after Thurtell joined her, the *Bellona* was uneventfully employed in home waters. There is no record of brave deeds in her logbooks, and she never fired a shot at an enemy or even chased a sail. Early in 1813 she was under orders to proceed in company with the *Theseus* and the *Niemen* to St Helena to pick up a convoy of East Indiamen returning with silks and spices. On 19 March she sailed with the other ships from the island, and after a fair passage the merchantmen dipped their ensigns to her in the Downs, and she went back to the Isle of Wight, dropping anchor off St Helen's.

For the next few months the ship was more actively employed; off Cape La Hogue and Barfleur and in the Basque Roads she frequently sighted the enemy and cleared for action. Soon after San Sebastian fell on 1 August 1813, the *Bellona* was cruising near that port (on the day it fell the muster was called at St Helen's, thus disproving the oft-repeated story of John's barbarous behaviour at the storming, to which, in indignant terms, he referred in his defence), and on 6 September she gave chase to two strange sail in heavy weather. They turned out to be a brig-of-war and a schooner, neither of which (a brig would only mount about sixteen small guns, and the schooner, if armed at all, would have carried a yet slighter armament) could offer fight. The brig made good her escape, but the schooner was boarded and made a prize. This brush with the enemy seems to have been the sole foundation for all John's subsequent talk, both in his fustian from the dock and in his yarns with George

Borrow of deeds of derring-do and moving incidents by flood and field.

Returning once more to the channel, the *Bellona* proceeded to Portsmouth, where she formed part of Admiral Bickerton's command until she was paid off about 22 February 1814, when Thurtell went on half-pay with temporary rank as second-lieutenant until he resigned his commission in June of that year.

No colour is given by the Marine Commissions List for 1814 to Borrow's suggestion (put into the mouth of Jack Dale in *The Romany Rye*) that 'he got into a scrape and lost his half-pay'. There is against his name nothing more than the words in red ink, 'Resigned his commission, June 1814.' Nothing appears against his conduct as an officer on the *Bellona*, and the captain gave him a good character at the trial; entirely mythical also is a story, circulated in *The Times* on 8 November 1823, that he was guilty of insubordination aboard the *Aboukir*.

Thurtell, still a minor, seems to have returned to Norwich and to have lived at home. Soon after he attained his majority his father, with ill-requited liberality, established him in business as a bombasine manufacturer in partnership with one Joe Giddens; and not much later he set up another son, Thomas, as a farmer in a considerable way, his rent being no less than £800 per annum. John's attention was greatly weaned from his business by the superior attractions of 'the fancy' and the society of raffish and disorderly persons. He became acquainted with two scamps named Bullen and Bagshawe, afterwards associated with him in frauds. He formed a more reputable friendship with the stout and straightforward pugilist, Ned Painter, nicknamed 'Flatnose', whose brawny person drew all the countryside on market days to The Anchor, in Lobster Lane, whither the champion removed in 1818 after his historic defeat of Tom Spring. Thurtell appears still to have been living with his parents, for it was at their house, it is said, that Borrow, then a boy in his teens, met him and learnt a little of sparring from him.

He seems to have formed an attachment, which his parents disapproved of, for a pretty Quakeress about this time, but his affection, though apparently reciprocated, cooled, and he formed a liaison with a local beauty (a native, perhaps, of Yarmouth) of no antecedents or education named Mary Dodson. He also became, during the year 1818 at latest, a frequent visitor to London, where his love of low company led him, to the great injury of his business, into the society not merely of questionable pugilists such as the Belascos, but of their backers, and of the gambling fraternity and the *chevaliers d'industrie* of the metropolis.

Among these sporting characters was the once noted Pierce Egan, who was present at the trial and very much in evidence at the execution of his crony. One of the worst of John's flash acquaintances was William Probert, a man of gigantic stature but of puny spirit, brazen and impudent when he conceived himself to be in safety; craven in a moment of real danger; of little education, but of much low cunning; plausible, well-dressed, a master of every species of roguery and cozenage, maintaining a smart gig, and displaying in the most embarrassed circumstances the unblushing front of the professional bankrupt. Some five years senior to John in age, and much richer as yet in every disreputable experience, he became the evil genius of his naturally vicious companion. Born in 1789 at Ross in Hertfordshire, the son of a respectable farmer, Probert, on his father's death (in consequence, as it was suggested in cross-examination, of a precocious inability to distinguish between *meum* and *tuum*), exchanged the quiet life of the farm for a stool in the office of a wine merchant named Bramwell, of Pimlico. A keen eye to his personal advantage led Probert to seek the hand of Miss Eliza Noyes, the affected and somewhat uncomely daughter of Mr William Crook Noyes, formerly an extensive brewer at Foxfield near Hungerford, and afterwards a farmer of his own freehold land at Tangley near Andover, whence he removed to Hampstead in very easy circumstances.

The lady was, it seems, several years her husband's senior,

but he received a 'handsome property' with her, whereby he was enabled to set up as a wine merchant on his own account in Coventry Street, with cellars hard by in the Haymarket. In 1818 he removed to 112 High Holborn, where he failed in July 1819 for £14,000, of which his creditors never received one penny. His solicitor in the bankruptcy proceedings was Mr Noel, afterwards prominently connected with the investigation of the historic murder, for the victim of which he had been acting.

Probert's method of conducting business was the 'long firm' one – to buy goods on credit, give bills for them, sell them for cash, and dishonour the bills at maturity. He was a pastmaster in the concealment of assets, and was committed to the King's Bench Prison for refusing to answer questions in his examination as a bankrupt. He remained there some two or three years, living extravagantly on the proceeds of secreted stock-in-trade – wines and spirits, which he sold for cash to the debtors, in fraud of his creditors, while contriving to hide with great cunning the notes and gold of which he thus became possessed on the occasions of the Commissioner's visits. He is said to have exceeded in the profligacy of his conduct even the ordinary debauchery of an inmate of a debtor's prison. After being enlarged under 'The Rules', he took the opportunity of robbing the coffee-room till of the King's Bench Prison of a considerable sum, for which offence he was tried at the sessions in Horsemonger Lane, and imprisoned for six months in the House of Correction at Brixton.

Meantime, Thurtell's visits to London became more frequent, and his neglect of his business accordingly increased.

I first became acquainted with John Thurtell [wrote Pierce Egan] by his occasional visits to the metropolis about the years 1818 or 1819, by accidentally meeting with him amongst other sporting characters at the various houses in London kept by persons attached to the sports of the field, horse racing, and the old English practice of boxing. . . . He was viewed as a young man of integrity.

Egan relates the decline of Thurtell's fortunes through neglect and dissipation and the circumstances immediately preceding his failure.

Thurtell came to London, it is said, to receive several hundred pounds for goods which he had sold to a respectable house in the city, and was on his return to pay the money amongst his creditors. On his return from London an account appeared in most of the newspapers that he had been attacked and cruelly beaten by foot-pads; but after a most desperate resistance on his part, he was compelled at the hazard of his life to part with his property to the robbers. It is a well-known fact that he appeared at Norwich terribly beaten, with a black eye and his head cut in several places. But his creditors insisted that it was a story propagated by Thurtell to deprive them of their property. . . . After this circumstance his character was gone in Norwich, and he therefore left it to be more at his ease in London. But reports injurious to his fame followed him to the metropolis; business was at an end, and how his time was occupied it would perhaps be difficult to describe.

The failure of Thurtell & Giddens was announced in *The Times* on 5 February 1821, meetings being called for 15, 16, and 17 March at the Norfolk Hotel, Norwich. On 30 October of the same year Thomas Thurtell, who had become heavily involved as a farmer and had 'disappeared' from Norwich, also failed under the description of 'licensed vic-tualler'. He subsequently made a composition with his creditors, for whom his father was by far the biggest.

On coming to town the brothers decided to tempt fortune in the *métier* of Boniface. John first established himself with May Dodson, his mistress, behind the bar at the Black Boy in Long Acre, which he took in the name of a younger brother, Henry, who subsequently 'went for a soldier'. He employed as manager in his absence a certain Cowdery, who afterwards gave evidence in favour of the County Fire Office in its proceedings against the Thurtells.

He established an ordinary and evening parties, which were attended by a great number of such persons as usually flock to houses of this description, all desirous of serving the landlord, for he had the name of being a good-humoured, affable, and social man. The principal attraction, however, was the handsome Miss D— [Dodson], who, as we have already stated, accompanied him in his disgraceful flight from Norwich, and now presided nominally as his barmaid, but was in reality his kept mistress.

The scenes of riot, dissipation, and annoyance constantly acted at this house led to a suspension of the licence, and thus in a very short time this public-house scheme proved abortive – the concern broke up, Miss D— was abandoned [this was not so], and Thurtell was again lost sight of in the vast chaos of crime and folly, of which the element in which he delighted to move was composed. (*The Fatal Effects of Gambling.*)

We hear that he used to frequent the Brown Bear in Bow Street, a great resort of the 'fancy', and the Army and Navy Tavern, kept by one Grieve, and subsequently for a brief period managed by Thurtell's infamous confederate Hunt.

By degrees he wormed himself into some intimacy with the champions of the ring, and for several years acted intermittently as a trainer and backer of pugilists. The first famous 'trial of manliness' with which he can unquestionably be identified was the historic encounter between his Norwich crony 'Ned Flatnose' and Tom Oliver, on 17 July, at North Walsham. Thurtell acted as backer of the local hero on this occasion, though in the press and in the *pugilistica* of the period he is not named, but described as a Norwich amateur. His connexion with the contest is familiar to all Borrovians. His application to a neighbouring magistrate for the loan of a 'pightle' lying among his broad acres, 'which he deemed would suit' as a milling ground, is one of the most familiar scenes in *Lavengro*; the author skilfully indicated by a few master strokes John's theatrical air and style of speech.

He was a man somewhat under thirty and nearly six feet high. He wore neither whiskers nor moustache, and appeared not to delight in hair, that is on his head, which was of a light brown, being closely cropped; the forehead was rather high, but somewhat narrow; the face was neither broad nor sharp, perhaps rather sharp than broad; the nose was almost delicate; the eyes were grey with an expression in which there was sternness blended with something approaching to feline; his complexion was exceedingly pale, relieved, however, by certain pockmarks, which here and there studded his countenance; his form was athletic, but lean; his arms long. In the whole appearance of the man there was a blending of the bluff and the sharp. You might have supposed him a bruiser; something, however, was wanting in his manner – the quietness of the professional man; he rather looked like one performing the part – well, very well – but still performing the part.

The description of this fight in *Lavengro* conveys the idea that it was a great 'Cross', Oliver suffering himself to be vanquished for vile lucre, and suddenly sinking 'to the earth before a blow of by no means extraordinary power'. . . . 'Tom has sold us' (said the fighting men from Town), 'sold us to the yokels.'

Whatever may have been Borrow's personal view, the best accounts of the battle accord far better with the jockey's eulogium of the dead man in *The Romany Rye* – 'He never bribed Tom Oliver to fight cross, as it was said he did on the day of the awful thunderstorm. Ned Flatnose fairly best Tom Oliver, for though Ned was not what's called a good fighter, he had a particular blow, which, if he could put it in, he was sure to win.'

'Some sharp blows passed,' says Miles in his *Pugilistica*, 'when Painter followed Oliver to the ropes, where the latter received a tremendous blow on his temple that floored him. When time was called, he could not appear at the scratch. . . . Oliver has declared since . . . that the blow operated on him like a shock of lightning, rendering him totally insensible.'

The victor drove away through the gathering storm in an open barouche – the favourite carriage of the 'fancy' – with postillions in scarlet jackets and Thurtell by his side, his features wearing a smile of triumph as he nodded to Borrow, while the 'smoking steeds' dashed through the crowd and scattered it, and the gipsy Pentulengro prophesied his 'bloody dukkeripen'.

The fight had drawn enormous numbers of sporting characters to Norwich, among whom were the pugilists Abe Belasco and Josh Hudson. Anecdotes connecting Thurtell with these personages and with others are to be found in the chronicles of the time. They illustrate the mixture of the the bluffer and the bully, which made up his unlovely character.

Back in London Thurtell again frequented the Brown Bear, and there became acquainted with Mr William Weare, a Mr Lemming or Lemon, a 'Captain' Elliott, and several other *chevaliers d'industrie*, who lived by blind hooky, hazard, billiards, and the promotion of crooked fights.

Weare, so far from being a solicitor or a man of education, as has been represented, was an ex-waiter from the Globe Tavern in Fleet Street, who later filled the same office at the gaming house. Having saved a considerable sum, and having a natural proficiency in billiards, he became, after acting for a time as marker, an independent player at the game, also attending race meetings, fights, spas, and seaside resorts with a variety of traps to catch unwary pigeons. He was at this time one of a gang of forty sharpers frequenting the gambling hells of the metropolis. It was his peculiarity to mistrust banks to such an extent that he preferred to carry his savings – no less than £2,000 – about his person in the form of notes, rather than keep an account. Mr Noel, his attorney, persuaded him to open an account at Morland's with £500, but he speedily closed it.

'I knew the victim well,' wrote John Payne Collier, 'having played hundreds of games of billiards with him. He was a regular blackleg, and was content to do business in a small way, if he could get no larger prey. So, as he was a good player, he used to earn a few shillings from me, who never risked more.' The billiard saloon keeper swore, according to some reports, that Weare was not a good player.

He had, however, a natural love of open-air sports, was a keen shot, and was devoted to dogs, of which he kept several in his rooms in Lyon's Inn. In person he was neat in attire, but far from attractive in features; he was diminutive in stature, 'had much of the cunning look of a Jew, and there was a peculiar hardness in his physiognomy; his cheek bones stood out so much and his chin was so small and pointed that his face below the eyes was quite a triangle'. He had an elder brother, a seedsman at Coventry; another, Richard, was a tailor in Southwark; and he is said to have had a third, who played *Macbeth* in Dublin on the night of the murder.

Weare, Thurtell, and several others were in the habit of going down to Wade's Mill, in Hertfordshire, for the purpose of training pugilists and of gaming at night. Thurtell lived profusely, drove down in post-chaise and four, and was accompanied by a mistress, a young woman of twenty-two of a fine, full figure, an East Anglian of somewhat free manners and of no too exquisite modesty.

Thurtell generally lost to Weare at play, in which he had little skill, but both were always ready to meet and pluck any local pigeons. Hickman, the 'Gasman', and Jack Martin, the 'Master of the Rolls', were two of Thurtell's intimates at this place, and he is said to have impersonated the latter pugilist (shortly after his defeat by Randall on Crawley Downs) at the benefit of Jack Carter, the 'Lancastrian Hero', some sixty miles from town. Finding the veteran in some distress, Thurtell proposed to secure a good gate by pretending to be the redoubtable Martin; the fraud was seen through by a London rider, but Thurtell resorted to his usual tactics, carrying off a desperate situation by intimidating the horseman by a show of bravado.

The second fight between Randall and Martin is said to have been a 'cross' arranged by Weare and his flash friends to appease Thurtell for his losses at play at the Mill. 'An attempt', says a scurrilous publication, 'was at first made to buy over Randall, but that pugilist was proof against all their offers, and their attention was next turned to Martin, with whom ... they succeeded. One bet was made of 1,100 to 600 guineas, and Thurtell had his share of the 600 guineas.' This fight, which took place on 16 September 1821, in the presence of 20,000 spectators, seems to have been a fair battle, in which the better man won. Little is to be read of our hero's share of the proceedings. 'Tom Spring and Mr Thurtle picked up Martin, and the whole party sported the radical castor (being white).' The 'castor' was the beaver tall hat of the period and the 'fancy' affected a white one, such as Thurtell was wearing on the morning after the murder. After one round, in which he suffered severely, Martin, who was trained much too fine in expert opinion, fell insensible against one of the stakes, and was unconscious for half an hour. Egan tells us that Thurtell, though in reality second to Martin, out of respect to his friends had himself described as an amateur; and in the *Pugilistica* it is stated that 'Tom Spring and an amateur were seconds for "The Master of the Rolls". Paddington Jones and "Cicero" Holt officiated for Randall.'

On his way down to the next great fight in which he was interested Thurtell had, as a companion on the coach, the famous critic, William Hazlitt. This was the historic battle between Hickman, 'The Gasman', and Bill Neat, fought on 11 December 1821, on Hungerford Downs.

Tom Thurtle, the trainer, sat before me on the coach-box, with whom I exchanged civilities as a gentleman going to the fight. When I got inside at Reading I found Thurtell and a stout valetudinarian, whose costume bespoke him as one of the 'fancy', and who had risen from a three months' sick bed ... to see the fight. They were intimate, and we fell into a lively disclosure. My friend the trainer was confined in his topics to fighting men and dogs, to bears and badgers – beyond this he was quite 'chapfallen', had not a word to throw at a dog, and indeed very wisely fell asleep when any other game was started. The whole art of training (I learnt from him) consists in two things ... exercise and abstinence – abstinence and exercise – repeated alternately and without end. ... Martin trains on water, but this increases his infirmity on another very dangerous side. ... Thurtell, starting out of his sleep, swore he knew how the fight would go, for he had had a dream about it. Sure the rascal told us how the first three rounds went off, but his dream denoted a 'foregone conclusion'. He knew his men.

Whatever may have been Hazlitt's opinion, this fight was no foregone conclusion; the result took the sporting world greatly by surprise. 'The Gasman' started a warm favourite, and his downfall resulted in 'A pretty "cleaning out" of the Londoners, who returned to town with "pockets to let". Nevertheless, there was little grumbling, all concurring in the general opinion that Hickman was entitled to praise, doing all that he could to win.'

There is a *verve* about old-time sporting reports, which brings back the days of *Rodney Stone* and the breezy, brutal life of the Regency and Georgian era :

Round 7 – Still Hickman seemed lively, but he was floored in a pig's whisper by a hit that drew his cork in profusion.
Round 10 – Neat ... received a nobber and returned one, two hard, which floored 'Gas' rudely.

Overtaken, it may be, by disaster which had befallen the 'Londoners', Thurtell seems henceforth to have renounced the ring. Except for the spar with Carter, when he posed as Martin, John Thurtell never fought a battle with any pugilist of note. Once, indeed, he challenged Tom Belcher for £500 a side, but on that veteran inviting him at the Fives' Court to make good his words by a glove battle then and there (explaining that he had retired from the prize ring) Thurtell remained silent, and his want of pluck was the subject of general comment. He equally displayed the white feather when challenged by Josh Hudson for some insulting remarks about his lack of fistic skill. This was the boxer to whom he had at a foregathering of sporting men at a Norwich hotel, after the fight at North Walsham, offered £5 to thrash Abe Belasco for suggesting that he had bribed Israel Belasco to fight a cross with the 'Berghampton Groom'. Abe's answer was to prophesy that he would live to see Jack hanged. After a little circulation of liquor, Hudson and the

Jew had a trial of manliness on the spot without the formality of seconds, each agreeing to discontinue the fight after receiving severe punishment.

It now became necessary to seek another means of livelihood than was offered by the patronage of the ring. John Thurtell was at this time an uncertificated bankrupt; but his brother Tom, though he had failed for £4,466, had made a composition of his creditors, of whom the chief was his father for £2,578, and, after some confinement on a collusive suit brought by his brother, had obtained the liberty of the 'Rules'. Somehow or other, and perhaps through the influence with the trade of the rascally Probert, Tom became, in 1822, the licensee of the Cock Tavern, Haymarket, where he installed his brother as manager. The two rogues also determined to run a 'long firm' business, a department of commerce in which their friend Probert was an expert. Accordingly towards the close of 1822 they raised money on bills – £500 being lent by their father – and bought a quantity of such goods as John had been accustomed to handle in Norwich – bombasines, Norwich crapes, and other silk goods. Most of these, Tom's credit being low, were bought for cash in London of the wholesale house, Todd, Morrison & Co. and Leaf & Co., also of Henry Dawson, of Norwich, and R. A. Dawson, of Leeds. These were all most respectable firms. Invoices for goods were later on produced by the Thurtells purporting to show purchases by them of like articles from their Norwich cronies Bullen and Bagshawe, but these, it was suggested, were merely designed to cloak the frauds, which will now be traced.

Tom had already, before Michaelmas of this year, taken part of the premises of Joshua Penny, wine merchant, of 93 Watling Street, ostensibly as a warehouse for the bombasine goods. Yet evidence given later, and Tom's own admissions, showed that the goods received were taken elsewhere, to William Steadman's, in Cumberland Street, New Road, and for the most part speedily disposed of for cash, at a loss of twenty per cent, to the firm of Margrave & Co., a certain

Snowden (a confederate of the brothers) acting as agent in these sales.

Such trading could have no honest purpose, and when it was stated that the supposed stock at Watling Street was insured, before any actual purchase, for nearly £200 in December 1822, and that the premises were completely gutted by fire on 26 January following, the thorough moral degeneracy of the brothers becomes too patent for the most adroit apologist to explain away.

That both brothers were equally involved is unquestionable, though the controlling mind was John's. Until shortly before the fire he had been sleeping at the warehouse with Mary Dodson. During this time he supervised the carrying out of certain structural alterations, which would have greatly impeded the utility of the premises as a warehouse, but were admirably adapted to conceal any act of arson from overlooking windows. These operations and the disturbance caused by them were no sooner over than John withdrew with his mistress to a house hard by on Garlick Hill – a very unsavoury neighbourhood. He lodged here at the house of a Mrs Amanda Gwillim, a lady whose accommodating nature and catholicity of view led her to let apartments for any length of time (counsel in cross-examination even suggested half an hour) to married couples, whose marriage lines she was too well-bred, too liberal-minded, and too confiding to inquire about. Moreover, she added in the witness-box, 'I am not to run to all the churches in London to look for registers of marriages.' I am pained to add that John Thurtell (nicknamed 'The Bully' and also 'Old Flare'), shortly after the fire, assaulted this pattern of her sex, for which she prosecuted him at the Guildhall. The issue of the case is not reported. The weapon of attack was a candlestick; perhaps the alderman applied the maxim, *De minimis non curat lex*, and dismissed the complaint. In consequence of this rupture, John withdrew from Mrs Gwillim's, and with Mary Dodson took up his residence once more at the Cock Tavern.

The County Fire Office, with whom the premises had been insured, immediately disputed liability. Thomas issued a writ against Mr Barber Beaumont, a director of the concern, and others, and the case came before Mr Justice J. A. Park at the sittings after term at the Guildhall on 25 June 1823.

This celebrated judge, so intimately connected with Thurtell's fate, was a lawyer of the old school, with prejudices of the oldest. He was singularly like His Majesty George III, a fact of which he was proud. He was well versed in the more abstruse branches of the profession, and was generally respected by the public and the bar. One of his chief prejudices was the traditional one of the English bench against Jews and Papists. Another was a very unprofessional one against port and potations, and he was not always able to subdue these prejudices, even when a display of them was inopportune. Deeply but narrowly religious, hot-tempered, irritable, and rather old-womanish, with much self-complacency and a full share of that judicial simplicity which affects not to know the slang of the day – such as the cant word for money, be it 'blunt' or 'oof' – the judge was sometimes led by his failings into ludicrous positions. Once, examining a little girl on the *voire dire* to see if she had the capacity to give evidence, he sought to test her knowledge of right and wrong in the customary manner with reference to the awful truths of Christian eschatology and the duty of every good child to offer up its nightly prayers. 'What do you do, my little maid,' he kindly asked, beaming to her with all the animation of his lively countenance, 'just before you get into bed?' Confusion reigned in the maiden's cheeks. A more worldly-wise man would here have put a 'leading question'. Sir Alan merely repeated his, and got the answer that everyone but himself was expecting.

To any movement or disturbance in Court he was notoriously sensitive, and when the disorder in the Town Hall at Hertford culminated in whistles from the gallery reserved for magistrates, Park's Christian forbearance, of which he was wont complacently to speak, must have been tried to its limit. Of his summing-up a learned contemporary wrote, 'He is rather happy at summing-up evidence; he seizes the leading points with considerable facility, and is successful in placing them clearly before the minds of the jury. Even in his decisions you see the self-complacency of the man. He scarcely ever delivers a judgment without some special reference to his "experience on the bench".'

In Thomas Thurtell's action against the fire office, Serjeant Lens was for the plaintiff and 'Brother Taddy' for the defendants. The onus, of course, lay upon them, yet they might have succeeded if their counsel had not turned the learned judge against him by creating a breeze in Court, in which the judicial dignity suffered a complete capsize. The scene, as described in *The Times*, may be quoted as an example of bygone forensic manners, and as an amusing exhibition of Sir Alan's foibles.

Taddy was cross-examining.

MR JUSTICE PARK: That is an improper question, and ought not to be put.

MR SERJEANT TADDY: That is an imputation to which I will not submit. I am incapable of putting an improper question to a witness.

MR JUSTICE PARK: What imputation, sir? I desire that you will not charge me with casting imputations, I say the question was not properly put, for the word 'disappear' means to leave clandestinely.

MR SERJEANT TADDY: I say it means no such thing.

MR JUSTICE PARK: I hope I have some understanding left; and so far as that goes, the word certainly bore that interpretation, and was therefore improper.

MR SERJEANT TADDY: I will never submit to a rebuke of this kind.

MR JUSTICE PARK: That is a very improper manner, sir, for counsel to address the bench.

MR SERJEANT TADDY: And that is a very improper manner for a judge to address counsel.

MR JUSTICE PARK (*rising in some warmth*): I protest, sir, you will compel me to do that which is disagreeable to me.

MR SERJEANT TADDY (*with equal warmth*): Do what you like, my lord.

MR JUSTICE PARK (*resuming his seat*): Well, I hope I shall manifest the indulgence of a Christian judge. (*A fatally foolish move, leading to a speedy checkmate.*)

MR SERJEANT TADDY: You may exercise your indulgence or power in any way your lordship's discretion may suggest; it is a matter of perfect indifference to me. I am ready to submit to whatever measure you may choose to adopt.

MR JUSTICE PARK: I have the function of a judge to discharge, and in doing so I must not be reproved in this kind of way.

MR SERJEANT TADDY: And I have a duty to discharge as counsel, which I shall discharge as I think proper, without submitting to a rebuke from any quarter.

(MR SERJEANT LENS *rose to interfere*.)

MR SERJEANT TADDY: No, brother Lens, I must protest against this interference.

MR SERJEANT LENS: My brother Taddy, my lord, has been betrayed into some warmth.

MR SERJEANT TADDY (*pulling Mr Serjeant Lens back into his seat*): I am quite prepared to answer for my own conduct.

MR JUSTICE PARK: My brother Lens has a right to be heard.

MR SERJEANT TADDY: Not on my account, my lord, I am fully capable of answering for myself.

MR JUSTICE PARK: Has he not a right to possess the Court on any subject he please?

MR SERJEANT TADDY: Not while I am in possession of the Court, and I am now examining a witness.

Here his Lordship threw himself back in his chair and remained silent.

But Taddy scored a pyrrhic victory, for, despite the cynical effrontery with which John Thurtell gave his evidence, inspiring the worthy judge with feeling that 'he was in the lowest state of degradation in point of moral feeling', Park revenged himself, as a weak judge worsted in a scene is too apt to do, by summing up dead against Taddy's clients, and the jury, without the least hesitation, returned a verdict for the plaintiff for £1,900. Gravely dissatisfied with the verdict, Mr Barber Beaumont at once caused an indictment to be prepared against the Thurtells and others for conspiracy to defraud the office. Proceedings were also taken as soon as the new term began to obtain a new trial, no execution issuing meantime on the judgment.

All this while Thomas Thurtell's affairs were in the hands of his assignees for the benefit of his creditors. Hence no immediate pecuniary advantage was gained by the brothers through these dealings, beyond the cash which the goods fetched at Margrave's, for although these sales represented a loss of twenty per cent, it must be remembered that it was borrowed capital raised on bills that the goods had been bought from Todd, Morrison, and others. The bills were not met at maturity, and the financial situation of the brothers thus became more and more involved.

John Thurtell was not, however, without resources; among the disreputable associates of Weare was a certain Lemming or Lemon, described in *Bell's Life* (23 November 1832), as 'The moneyed employer of Thurtell and others in their diabolical practices.' This man was a master of roguery in all its departments; with a gang of blacklegs and sharpers he visited spas and watering-places to fleece the unwary. In the year 1823 some of the gang were operating in Kent, making Margate their headquarters.

Weare operated at Bath during the season of this year, and was at Doncaster in September for the St Leger meeting, doubtless taking with him his paraphernalia of gaming.

The Army and Navy Tavern, one of Thurtell's houses of call, had lately changed hands. Mr Grieve, who had been the proprietor, gave up the house, and a widow took it over, entrusting the management of it to one Joseph Hunt, who thus became acquainted with the man with whose name his own has ever been associated in the chronicles of infamy. Hunt's early history is obscure. He was about twenty-six years of age in 1823, had already been confined in Newgate – on what charge cannot be ascertained – and, though evidently a man of the slenderest education, had some respectable connexions by marriage, one sister being married to a

Captain O'Reilly, of the Australian service. A brother of his was a singer at Covent Garden Theatre, and Joseph himself was as good a vocalist as a semi-literate man could reasonably be. He visited seaside places during the season, earning trifles by his voice, and was well known at Brighton. Though an arrant coward as well as a rogue, he seems to have assisted Thurtell and the gang he worked with in those occasional scrimmages in the gambling halls, which resulted from the sharper's method of play. As landlord of the Army and Navy Tavern his career was short and inglorious. He failed to pay for goods delivered at the house, and decamped considerably in debt and with no honest means of livelihood before him. The affairs of the Thurtells were also desperate. The butcher, who supplied the Cock with meat, cut off their credit early in 1823, they owing him some £11. They had also been obliged to realize the contents of the cellar, and had bills to the amount of about £900 falling due. Thomas, when later he was in custody, said that he had paid several hundred pounds' worth of acceptances forged by his brother during this year, in order to save him from being hanged. It is difficult, however, to reconcile this assertion with his own insolvency at the time.

Such were the circumstances of these hardened villains when Weare returned to town in October 1823, laden with the spoils of the Doncaster meeting. Having fled from the Cock, not merely because of the ruin of their affairs, but for the cogent reason that, being unable to find bail in the matter of the pending prosecution by the County Fire Office, they were momentarily apprehensive of arrest, the brothers took up their lodging in this month at the Coach and Horses, Conduit Street, kept by Charles Tetsall, a friend of Probert. The wine merchant's affairs were also very involved. Soon after his enlargement from the King's Bench, he had obtained a lease of £35 a year of a cottage at Gill's Hill, near Elstree, where he ran a 'jigger', or illicit still. As the discharge of his pecuniary obligations never troubled Mr Probert, he was under notice to leave, not having paid any rent.

Weare soon after his return to town began to frequent his old haunts. A favourite billiard saloon with him was William Rexworthy's in Spring Gardens, where a new table had just been installed. The proprietor saw him several times at his house with John Thurtell, Hunt, and Probert during some ten days before his disappearance on 24 October. On the previous day, a Thursday, Weare had been at the saloon in company with John Thurtell, and had then informed Rexworthy of his intention of going into Hertfordshire with his companion next day for a few days' shooting.

The attention of the magistracy was first directed to the disappearance of Weare by Charles Nicholls, of Batler's Green, Aldenham, a farmer, who informed the Watford bench, at their petty sessions on Tuesday, 28 October 1823, of some singular circumstances pointing to foul play. The justices, acting under the old statutes, proceeded to hold a criminal investigation. Mr Clutterbuck in particular was active. He at once repaired to a part of Gill's Hill Lane, where a murder was said to have been committed, and conducted an investigation on the spot, which resulted in the immediate arrest of Probert. Having no efficient local constabulary, only unpaid parish constables, he summoned professional aid from London, and two 'robin redbreasts', as the Bow Street Runners were called because of their scarlet waistcoats, came down next day – Simmonds and Ruthven. Continuing their inquiries, the local magistrates ordered the arrest of both the Thurtells and of Hunt. The examinations of many witnesses were taken at the house of Nicholls, the informant, and lasted until three o'clock in the morning of Wednesday, 28 October, when the exhausted justices returned home.

By five that afternoon Ruthven had arrived again from town, having laid both Hunt and John Thurtell by the heels. The singularly callous demeanour of both ruffians was in later years described by the famous runner to 'Chief Baron' Nicholson, who has preserved the account in his reminiscences :

While upon the subject I may as well give George Ruthven's account, which I have received from his own lips, of the apprehension of Thurtell and the others concerned in that horrible murder. 'After it had been ascertained that it was human blood [no test at that time could detect human blood as distinct from mammalian] and human hair upon the pistol, and Hunt and Probert were in custody, I left in order to secure John Thurtell. I found him at the Coach and Horses, Conduit Street, Hanover Square. I said: John, my boy, I want you. What do you want, George? he said. I replied, Never mind, I'll tell you presently. Thurtell had been anticipating serious proceedings against him for setting his house on fire in the city, by Mr Barber Beaumont, of the County Fire Office. It was highly probable that he supposed that I wanted him on that charge. He however prepared to accompany me. My horse and chaise were at the door. He got in and I handcuffed him to one side of the rail of my trap. I drove on towards Hertford [probably Watford]. On the road nothing could be more chatty and free than the conversation on the part of Thurtell. If he did suspect where I was going to take him, he played an innocent part very well, and artfully pretended total ignorance. We had several glasses of grog on the road. When we arrived, I drove up to the inn, where Probert and Hunt were in charge of the local constables. Let us have some brandy and water, George, said Thurtell, after he had shaken hands with his associates. I went out of the room to order it. Give us a song, said Thurtell, and Hunt, who was a beautiful singer, struck up 'Mary, list wake.' I paused with the door in my hand and said to myself – Is it possible that these men are murderers?'

The magistrates recommenced their inquiries at the Essex Arms Inn, after having first received Mr Noel, Weare's solicitor (formerly Probert's), and Rexworthy, who informed them of Weare's disappearance and of his avowed intention of going on a shooting expedition with John Thurtell. Rexworthy, Philip Smith, James Freeman, and his wife (who was not called at the trial), John Herrington, Richard Hunt, Nicholls, William Bulwer, Susan Woodroffe, James Addis, and Ruthven were all examined, and gave substantially the same testimony that each repeated at the trial. The prisoners, under the old Tudor procedure, were not allowed to be confronted with the witnesses against them, but when the examinations were over were themselves subjected to a searching interrogation, based upon the information taken behind their backs.

Hunt seems at first to have said nothing. The accounts, however, vary. Jones, who was present, says, 'Thurtell, Hunt, and Probert, were called in and examined.' Thurtell's examination (which might have been put in and proved against him, although, in fact, it was not) exhibits the usual lies and evasions, by which a prisoner, ignorant of what had been deposed against him, usually entrapped himself. *The Times* (1 November 1823) thus reports what passed :

John Thurtell was then called in and examined. His account of the transaction differed very materially from that given by Hunt. He said he had no appointment with a gentleman to go down with him on that night. Took up no gentleman on the road. Never told any one that he could take him for a day's shooting. He walked with Probert and Hunt on Saturday in the lane for about ten minutes. They all had black hats on. His clothes and boots were not so dirty as to require a great deal of brushing on Saturday morning. The scratches on his hands were partly caused by some brambles, while he was shooting, and partly by the bite of a dog. He never said anything to Mr Hunt or any one else about his hands being scratched.

He was next pressed as to his acquisition of a pistol found upon him by Ruthven, and while he was offering his explanation he was suddenly confronted with the companion to it.

The pistol with the blood and hair adhering to it was then slowly exposed to the view of the prisoner ... and his countenance and manner underwent a change too striking to escape the notice of the most careless observer. His complexion, naturally sallow, assumed a deadly pallor, and he appeared to shudder and shrink backward at the sight of the weapon.

This was the pistol found in the lane near the scene of the struggle with Weare. The purchase of the pair was proved at the trial by a witness, Cogswell, in the employ of a pawnbroker named Hall. The youth was certain of the date of the purchase, 24 October, of the day of the murder, and of the identity of the weapons, but could only give a general description of the purchasers as a tall man and a shorter one, which well agreed with the persons of Thurtell and Hunt.

No one could reasonably doubt that the three accused had made away with Weare; but an obstacle stood in the way of their conviction which might prove insuperable – no one knew where the body was, except the accused themselves. The general belief was that it had been carried to town and thrown into the Thames. If not speedily discovered, decomposition would destroy all chance of identification – in this dilemma it became imperative to induce one of the three to turn approver. Hunt was first approached very irregularly by Mr Noel, Weare's solicitor, who, without authority, promised him his life. His natural pusillanimity rendered the task easy. He was soon convinced that if he did not confess one or other of his accomplices would. He accordingly made a confession, in which he carefully suppressed the extent of his own guilt, but gave the Crown the supremely important information sought, that is, the situation of the body.

When he had finished it was nine o'clock in the morning of 30 October; the justices, who had been engaged all night, decided to adjourn until persons deputed for that purpose had searched the pond – called Hill's Slough – indicated by Hunt as concealing the victim. Joseph Johnston and others forthwith accompanied Hunt to the spot, some three miles from Probert's cottage, and after some difficulty, drew forth from the shallow water a nude corpse, around the trunk of which had been wrapped a sack. This ghastly object the searchers carried to the Artichoke Inn at Elstree. The discovery being reported to the bench, they immediately committed John Thurtell for the murder at the forthcoming special Gaol Delivery in December.

On the next day, Friday, 31 October, Benjamin Rooke, the coroner, held an inquisition *super visum corporis*, and Hunt and Probert were brought into the room. Hunt was silent, but Probert declared, 'I never saw the corpse before.

I declare to God, I never did; you may rely on it, I never saw that unhappy man before.'

Rexworthy and other witnesses were again examined, and some amplified their testimony already given by the addition of minor facts – as is commonly the case. Mr Ward, a surgeon of Watford, proved the cause of death, and minutely described the injuries from the discharge of the pistol, the blows with the butt of it, and from the knife. He added, 'The teeth of the upper jaw were forced out, and the mouth otherwise mutilated.' Ruthven proved finding a number of Weare's things in Hunt's lodgings, and Bates, a boy, proved the finding among some dung in Probert's stable of a shirt marked 'W' corresponding in every way with those found in Hunt's possession. Ruthven now intimated to the bench that Probert wished to say something. Two of the justices went into the room where he was; the craven giant, very characteristically, fell upon his knees in the attitude of prayer, and said, 'I declare in the presence of my Maker I never saw the man; I never knew the man, so help me God!'

After the usual formalities the inquest was adjourned till next day, and the prisoners were committed to St Alban's gaol. At the resumed proceedings many persons were called, including the Justice's clerk, Jones, who has left us the most reliable report of the case, He was present when Weare's body was taken from the sack, and thus describes its appearance – 'The hands were crossed on the chest ... under each armpit was a large flint stone; the legs were also crossed and tied with a cord, which confined the sack round the body.'

After further evidence Hunt was called in and made a confession, not differing in essentials from what he had already given to the magistrates, but considerably more detailed. In each confession he pretended to have had no previous knowledge of any murderous design, and no personal share in the disposal of the remains in Hill's Slough. He was then sharply questioned by the coroner as to his share of the booty, which he impudently maintained was a sum of £6 paid him under agreement with Probert as his professional fee for singing at the cottage on the night of the crime. But he was forced to admit that he had bought the cord and sack used to envelop the body at John Thurtell's request, and had given them to him; he pretended that he thought that the sack was to put game in. The purchase of the cord he did not attempt to explain. He denied having ever worn any of the deceased's clothes, which was palpably untrue. In short, he equivocated and lied on every matter, which brought home to him a guilty knowledge of Thurtell's intention. He signed his statement 'with the composure of a person engaged in the transaction of some business of an ordinary nature'.

Probert was next brought in. He unfolded a tale which, like Hunt's, departed widely from the truth in those particulars which bore upon his own guilt. He said nothing of handling or removing the body, of having seen it, or of knowing where it was. Eventually the coroner warned him to stop.

CORONER: If you take my advice, you will give us no more.

PROBERT: If you please, sir, I can only say that I am not a murderer. I never saw the man and I never knew his name; I declare to God... I am totally innocent of the murder. I did not know of the man's coming any more than the man in the moon. I declare to God my saviour, God Almighty knows I am not guilty.

He flatly contradicted Hunt's story that he had employed Hunt professionally to sing on the night of the murder.

The jury, dispensing with any summing up, found that 'John Thurtell, late of etc ... Gentleman, with a certain pistol of the value of ten shillings, charged and loaded with gunpowder and leaden slugs,' and 'with a certain iron and steel knife of the value of sixpence' in and upon one William Weare, in the presence of God and of our Lord the King, then and there being, did make an assault, and did kill him in the manner deposed by the surgeon, and that Joseph Hunt and William Probert, respectively 'gentleman' and 'wine merchant', counselled, procured, incited, and abetted the said John Thurtell the said murder and felony to do and commit. The two accomplices were at once conveyed to Hertford gaol, and Thomas Thurtell was also arrested on a warrant, charging him with conspiring to defraud the County Fire Office.

On 10 November Mr Serjeant Taddy moved for a new trial of *Thurtell v. Beaumont*, before Dallas, C. J., and Burrough, and Park, J. J. The intervening murder and the production of two affidavits, one sworn by Hunt in Hertford gaol, and detailing an alleged conversation with John Thurtell in which he admitted the arson at 93 Watling Street, were thought to have strengthened the hands of the serjeant not a little, and he took a rule *nisi*, returnable in the Hilary term following.

On 19 November, Mr Chitty, a lawyer who had the distinction of founding one of the best known of English legal families, and had, after many years of lucrative practice under the bar, been called in middle life, made two motions on behalf of the prisoner Thurtell. One was for a *mandamus* calling on the Hertford bench, as 'visiting justices', and the Governor of the gaol to admit to the prison under proper supervision and at all reasonable times Messrs Jay and Fenton, attornies for John Thurtell, in order that they might take instructions for his defence. The other was for a criminal information against Mr Williams, of the Surrey Theatre, and another, for a high misdemeanour in attempting to pervert the course of justice by exhibiting at the said theatre a play entitled *The Gamblers*, in which the whole story was enacted, as it had been fulsomely related in the public prints. Williams, 'in order to give great *éclat* to the performance, purchased the identical chaise in which the murder was committed or first attempted, and in which, it will be remembered, Thurtell drove Weare to the lonely cottage in Gill's Hill Lane.' The curious bald-faced horse, which had also been hired, and had been a dumb spectator of the crime, was likewise on view. The Court immediately granted the *mandamus*, and made a rule *nisi* in the other matter. The performance was withdrawn but was immediately resumed after the conviction in January following. On 28 November Mr Chitty obtained a rule absolute for a criminal information against Messrs Edgerley, Sherwood, and Jones, who had severally published accounts of the proceedings up to the date, calculated to pervert the course of justice.

On being informed of his arrest, Thomas Thurtell, who had an impediment in his speech, made several disclosures about his brother. 'He admitted that his brother had led a life the most wicked and dissolute for several years ... He stated that his brother had forged his acceptance to bills to the amount of £600 only eight months ago, and he was compelled to pay the money to save his life. ... He burst into tears, "Good God, what misery must my poor father and mother endure!"'

When the inquest had been concluded on Saturday, 1 November, night had fallen, but it was thought best to inter the remains without delay. They were accordingly conveyed in the darkness to Elstree churchyard, to repose near the nameless grave of the beautiful Miss Ray, the actress and erstwhile mistress of Jemmy Twitcher, the notorious Earl of Sandwich, who betrayed his crony Wilkes for publishing his *Essay on Woman*. She had fallen a victim to the pistol of a crazy parson named Hackman, who killed her to avenge a hopeless passion.

That nothing should be wanting to fill the cup of horror to the brim, the burial of the quondam waiter of The Globe was attended by a strange combination of sinister circumstances. It was eleven at night when the bell tolled for the ceremony. A few dim candles illuminated the church; by their feeble aid, the parson, with difficulty, mumbled the words of the service to a crowd of idle and disorderly persons, attracted merely by the same feelings which later drew unprecedented crowds to the murderer's doom. A half-dozen glimmering lanterns lighted the way to the grave. Tall trees surrounding the churchyard deepened the black pall of night. As the coffin was being lowered a rope round the foot of it broke, and the coffin fell into an upright position, men springing into the grave and struggling to settle it level.

The Times devoted five and a half columns of awesome description to the weird spectacle.

The scene which now presented itself as one which can never pass from the recollection of those who witnessed it. The unusual hour of the interment, the horrible manner in which the man whose corpse had just been consigned to the grave had lost his life, the solemn stillness of the night, for the wind, which had been loud and boisterous during the day, had now fallen ... the impressive nature of the beautiful and affecting composition which was read by the clergyman, who stood conspicuous in his white gown, whilst all around him was darkness, except where the feeble light of a lanthorn happened to fall on the countenance of some of the mourners – all these circumstances produced an effect on the beholders which, we think, can hardly be surpassed.

It was not long before the gravediggers repaired again to the churchyard – this time to exhume the corpse, in order that Bingham, an ostler at the White Lion, a house called at by Weare and Thurtell on the night of 24 October, might attempt to identify the remains.

The parties, who were to perform and witness the disinterment, repaired to the churchyard at midnight. The night was dark, and the weather most inclement. Storms of rain and hail assailed the individuals who had taken upon themselves the unpleasant task. ... By great exertions the coffin, which had been nearly full of water, was brought up; the lid was then unscrewed, and the corpse once more submitted to inspection. We forbear to enter into any minute description of the ghastly spectacle which now met the view when lights were brought close to the deceased. The secrets of the charnel house are too awful for the general perusal of those who yet live. ... It is sufficient to say that, when the contents of the coffin were looked upon, it was instantly obvious to every one that recognition was impossible. The lid of the coffin was then replaced, and the body was again lowered into the grave.

Two days after the funeral several more arrests were made. Probert's wife and one of her sisters, Miss Anne Noyes, a flippant, one-eyed, very uncomely person, who had both been at Gill's Hill during the time the corpse lay there, were apprehended by Bishop, a runner, in Castle Street, Leicester Fields. Thomas Noyes, a brother of the ladies, who had played cards at the cottage on the Sunday after the murder, was also taken. 'He was fearfully agitated, the perspiration flowed from him profusely, he struck his hands violently on his forehead, and appeared to be nearly choked in endeavouring to express his feelings.'

On Wednesday, 5 November, Mrs Probert disclosed the possession of a gold chain; it had been given her on the night of the murder by John Thurtell, as she subsequently proved; it had belonged to Weare.

Throughout the month the Hertford bench were pursuing their inquiries, taking depositions from several other witnesses besides the fifty-four finally examined in Court. Sir Richard Birnie, the chief magistrate of the metropolis, also conducted a magisterial investigation at Bow Street, for which, as well as for the assistance rendered by his Runners, he received the thanks of the local justices after the trial. In consequence of the information acquired by him in his investigations, Sir Richard instructed the Margate Police to effect the arrest of Lemon, who seems to have been a veritable Jonathan Wild, but the inefficient county constabulary of the period proved unequal to the task, and this dangerous ruffian escaped to the Continent. On 18 November Anne Noyes was liberated, and her brother was set free on the 29th having entered into recognizances in £100 and £200 respectively to attend and give evidence at the forthcoming trial.

Throughout the whole of November the daily and weekly press teemed with allusions to the case. Anecdotes of the early lives of the prisoners and of their victim, and of all associated in any way with the case, flooded the newspapers. *The Times* stood conspicuous for the manner in which it pandered to the morbid craving for any gossip about the ghouls of Gill's Hill. All sorts of crimes actually executed or merely contemplated were attributed to the prisoner John

Thurtell. Stories revealing the lowest depths of trickery and meanness were eagerly retailed about the other two. Persons of the highest consideration sought pretexts for interviews with the murderer himself. Among these was Sir Thomas Lawrence, P.R.A., who wished to take a cast of his head in the interests of the then fashionable science of phrenology. The Earl of Essex, accompanied by his footman, visited the gaol to see if he could recognize in the person of John Thurtell a mysterious ruffian who had waylaid him some little time before.

Meantime the commission day of the special gaol delivery drew near, with the public excitement daily increasing and imaginations of all ranks violently inflamed against the prisoners. Persons of quality and leisure hurried from the most distant corners of the kingdom to be present, and fought for seats on the coaches bound for Hertford. The roads were crowded with tilburies, chaises, barouches, and horsemen. On the commission day itself the High Sheriff of Hertfordshire set out with twenty javelin men and a considerable retinue of the county gentry to meet Sir George Holroyd and Sir Alan Park, the judges in the commission of gaol delivery, who were approaching Hertford from Lord Verulam's seat at Gorhambury, where they had stayed the previous night.

The Honourable William Lamb, afterwards Lord Melbourne, was foreman of the grand jury. Nobility and fashion crowded the little town. Women of the great world and women of the half-world jostled one another in the public taverns. The bald-faced horse, whose equine eyes had seen all, was an object of the greatest curiosity. The worst inn's worst room commanded any price for the night. The colossal Probert, on coming from the grand jury room, excited as much interest as 'The Duke' at a levee. A remarkable paper, 'A Late Trial at Hertford', in the *London Magazine* (February 1842), stated : 'The buzz of conversation amidst all and in all places was a low murmur but of "Thurtell", "Miss Noyes", "Probert", "Mrs Probert", and "Hunt". These vice-creatures were on all lips – and in no hour betwixt the evening and the morning was their infamy neglected to be told upon the night.'

After opening the commission and attending divine service, the judges adjourned to their lodgings, and in the afternoon returned to the Town Hall. Mr Justice Park took his seat in the Crown Court to charge the grand jury; while his able colleague, a man marked out by his fearless independence as pre-eminently fit to conduct a trial fairly in the teeth of prejudice, repaired to a second Court to deal with such minor cases as the grand jury might find. Park rose to the occasion; he was fully aware that all eyes were upon him. He had at all times an exaggerated sense of his importance to his country. 'He looks at everything,' said a contemporary, 'in which he is himself as a judge engaged, through a glass of prodigious magnifying capabilities.' He had, moreover, all the self-made man's worship of the artificial barriers of pedigree. To be surrounded at this moment by the rank and beauty of the country, and to be for the nonce the first amongst them, flattered the self-complacency of the judge in a manner which is amusingly apparent in his charge, not the less so for being disguised under an assumption of humility and of unworthiness worthy of a Heep, and, as Sir James Stephen has said, so characteristic as to guarantee the fidelity of the report. 'The language of reproach is never pleasant to me. . . . It is hostile to my feelings. . . . I am continually in error, for no human being can doubt that he errs continually, because he is a human being.' The learned judge concluded his charge by saying that if the three prisoners were tried on one indictment, the evidence of Mrs Probert would be altogether inadmissable. According to *The Times*, the effect of the judge's concluding words was for a fresh bill of indictment to be forthwith drawn omitting Probert, whom it had been determined to use as King's evidence, partly on account of the reservations in Hunt's confession, but also to introduce the testimony of Mrs Probert, which could not have been used against John Thurtell if Probert were in jeopardy of conviction.

However that may be, it is undoubted that Hunt and Thurtell were indicted together under the 'addition' of 'labourers', and that no indictment against Probert is extant; inasmuch as he stood charged as accessory before the fact upon the coroner's inquisition, it was needless to prepare a bill against him for the mere purpose of his formal acquittal. The grand jury found a true bill against Hunt and Thurtell, and on the following day, 5 December, all three prisoners were put to the bar, when Hunt and Thurtell pleaded to their indictment, and, together with Probert, pleaded not guilty to the inquisition.

The pleas taken, Mr Andrews, leading counsel for Thurtell, applied to the Court that certain affidavits might be sworn. They related to the campaign of calumny carried on in the Press, and especially in *The Times* itself, against the prisoners. After some discussion and certain formalities, the clerk of the Court proceeded to read an affidavit by Thurtell's attornies setting forth particulars of the libels in the papers and in the various publications in book form which had already appeared, as well as of the infamous performance at the Surrey Theatre. The reading concluded, Messrs Andrews, Platt (afterwards Mr Baron Platt), and Chitty moved for an adjournment, to which motion Mr Gurney (afterwards Mr Baron Gurney) offered no serious opposition. His reply is notable only for having drawn from the judge a repetition of the opinion he had so forcibly expressed in his charge – that it was most improper to acquaint a prisoner with the evidence against him.

After some further observations from Mr Andrews, Mr Justice Park adjourned the Court to eight o'clock in the morning of 6 January 1842, urging all persons 'within the sound of his voice' to 'disclaim and withhold such publications' as had been set out in the affidavits on the prisoner's behalf. This salutory warning, though it produced a little foolish abuse of the judge in the Press next day, completely put a stop to the scandals complained of. Mr Herbert, author of the very spirited account of the trial in the *London Maga-*

zine, has left an amusing description of the awe felt by certain humble fellow-passengers on the London coach, who were in guilty possession of authentic portraits and memoirs of the accused, from the sale of which they hoped for a profitable trade. When it was stated that *The Times* itself published, on 10 November, a detailed description of the attempt alleged to have been made on 7 October by John Thurtell to murder Mr Woods, some idea will be obtained of the spirit of journalism at this time. The fact that such publications were not dealt with as contempts of court, had, no doubt, much to do with their recklessness. 'Some very good likenesses of the pond', which had decorated the window of the Six Compasses, were forthwith withdrawn, under the motion that they were actionable.

On 4 December Thurtell had received two visitors at the gaol; one was the officer formerly commanding in Leith Roads, Sir Edmund Nagle, who had been served with a subpoena by Messrs Jay and Fenton, and had journeyed down from London to see if he could pick out the prisoner as one who had served under him, so as to speak as to his conduct. Nagle was, however, entirely unable to recollect the lieutenant of marines, but was satisfied by Thurtell recalling the names of shipmates and the circumstances of some entertainments on board the *Adamant* that he had at one time been under his command. The prisoner apologized to the Admiral for the unnecessary trouble to which he had been put, and the Admiral returned to town. The second visitor was the well-known sportsman Pierce Egan, who had known John for some five years. The demeanour of the prisoner, as described by Egan, who repeated his visit next day, was typical of the murderer – boastful, egoistic, impenitent, untruthful. His 'sullen, low love of fame' made his present notoriety not altogether displeasing. 'But what a piece of work this affair has made, ain't it? ... Do I appear dejected?' he remarked with evident glee. He showed, however, as he did at the end, a sense of the disgrace he had brought upon his parents.

EGAN: You have not been to see your father or mother for these two or three years past, I suppose?

THURTELL: Oh! yes I have (*giving a deep sigh*). It is not seven weeks ago since I dined with them at Norwich, in company with Mr Jay, my solicitor, at my father's house. [It was more than seven weeks since the murder.]

EGAN: Since you have been at Hertford, your father has not been to see you, nor any of your relations, have they?

THURTELL: No, no. I could not see my father. My feelings would not permit me. . . . I saw my brother Tom yesterday; that was quite enough for my feelings to undergo.

To the many persons who sought interviews out of mere curiosity Thurtell showed a pardonable coldness. It would be idle to recall such trifles but for the light they shed on social life just over a century ago.

As the adjourned date of trial drew near public excitement waxed once more. Many persons came even from Ireland, as well as from the most distant parts of Great Britain, in the vain hope of finding room in the Town Hall. The Press, which had for some weeks maintained a decent silence, then burst forth with redoubled activity. Every paper had four to six 'Horse Expresses'; it was calculated that there were not less than one hundred horses placed on the road for this purpose.

Ever since the arrest of Probert his wretched cottage had been an object of pilgrimage to thousands. The landlord, to whom the rent had been long owing, conceived the happy notion of charging a toll for admission. So great were his receipts that an unseemly squabble occurred between him and the Sheriff as to whether the gate-money belonged to the landlord by way of distress or to the Sheriff in lieu of execution, it being a case of *nulla bona*. According to Sir Walter Scott, John Bull 'became so maudlin . . . to treasure up the leaves and twigs of the hedge and shrubs in the fatal garden as valuable relics'.

In the town of Hertford itself hundreds were unable to secure sleeping accommodation. The *London Magazine* of February 1842 states:

Throughout the night [of Monday, 5 January] Hertford was as sleepless as before. The window at the Plough was as luminous as usual; the Half-Moon swarmed with post-chaises and drab coats; and the Seven Stars, the Six Compasses, and the Three Tuns abounded with tippling witnesses, all dressed in their Sunday clothes. . . . The Court was crowded to excess, and even at this early hour [7.30] the window panes, from the great heat, were streaming with wet.

The influx on the morning after the trial of a large number of fighting men, fresh from the great battle at Worcester between Spring and Langan, added to the turbulence of the town. The proceedings during the two days of the trial were constantly interrupted by disorderly outbreaks, which greatly tried the temper of the Court.

At eight o'clock the trumpets of the javelin men brayed the arrival of Mr Justice Park, who shortly afterwards entered the Court and took his seat. As usual, the Court was colloquial respecting the heat – and the crowd – and the sitting down of tall men – to the loss of much of that imposing dignity with which the ermine and the trumpets invariably surrounded the judge.

A long delay occurred; it was explained that the prisoners were having their irons removed.

In this interval, Mr Jay and Mr Fenton, attornies for the prisoner Thurtell, were struggling to find their way through the crowd for the purpose of obtaining places near the prisoner's counsel, and, having reached the point intended, and there being great noise and confusion in the effort, Mr Justice Park inquired who were the persons thus increasing the disturbance. Mr Fenton and Mr Jay respectfully intimated that they were the attornies in the case. Mr Justice Park replied, with considerable warmth, 'Nonsense, it is only to make a fuss; you ought to be here in the morning.'

After further ebullitions from the bench, the prisoners at length made their appearance. Mr Herbert thus describes the scene in the *London Magazine* :

Hunt was dressed in black with a white cravat and a white handkerchief carefully disposed so as to give the appearance of a

48

white under-waistcoat. There was a foppery in the adjustment of this part of his dress which was well seconded by the affected carriage of his head and shoulders and by the carefully disposed *disorder* of his hair. It was combed forward over his ears from the back part of his head and divided nicely on his forehead so as to allow one lock to lie half-curled upon it. His forehead itself was white, feminine, and unmeaning; indeed his complexion was extremely delicate, and looked more so from the raven blackness of his hair. Nothing could be weaker than his features, which were small and regular, but destitute of the least manly expression. . . . Beside him stood the murderer, complete in frame, face, eye, and daring! The contrast was singular – fatal, indeed, to the opinion which it created of Thurtell. He was dressed in a plum-coloured frock coat with a drab waistcoat and gilt buttons and white corded breeches. His neck had a black stock on, which fitted as usual stiffly to the bottom of the cheek and end of the chin, and which therefore pushed the flesh on this part of the face so as to give an additionally sullen weight to the countenance. The lower part of the face was unusually large, muscular, and heavy, and appeared to hang like a load to the head and to make it drop like a mastiff's jowel. The upper lip was long and large, and the mouth had a dogged appearance. His nose was rather small for such a face, but it was not badly shaped. His eyes were too small, and buried deep under his protruding forehead, so indeed as to defy you to detect their colour. The forehead, extremely strong, bony, and knotted – and the eyebrows were forcibly marked though irregular – that over the right eye being nearly straight, and that over the left turning up to a point, so as to give a very painful expression to the whole face. . . . His frame was exceedingly well knit and athletic. . . . I have observed that Thurtell seldom looked at the person with whom he conversed . . . but looked straight forward.

Probert was subsequently brought in and placed in the dock, but not close to the bar, gaolers interposing between him and the other two. Mr Thesiger, distinguished in later life as Lord Chelmsford, who had been called to Gray's Inn just over five years before, now rose to move the adjournment of Hunt's trial. Lengthy affidavits had been prepared on both sides, and, after argument, Mr Justice Park overruled the application and ordered the trial to proceed. There at once occurred one of those comical scenes – recurring throughout the proceedings – in which human nature, having supped full of horrors, found relief in laughter. Several burly jurymen, after having taken up comfortable seats in the box, were challenged by the defence, and reluctantly compelled to withdraw. After twelve had been sworn, the Clerk of Assize charged them both on the indictment and the inquisition, and then the craven Probert was formerly acquitted. Fear and worry had largely blanched his raven black hair since his first apprehension, and the pencil of Mulready, busily employed throughout the trial, seems to to have caught the alteration of his appearance. The sketches of Probert made by Mulready appear to have been made on various occasions. In most the hair is blanched; in one or two it is black. When tried for horse-stealing in June 1820 Probert, according to *The Times*, had quite white hair. *The Fatal Effects* tells us that 'his hair was turning grey' at the date of Thurtell's trial.

After a formal opening of the indictment, now disused, Mr Gurney addressed the jury on behalf of the Prosecution. His speech was 'slow, distinct, and concise. In several of the most appalling parts of his statement there was a cold drawing in of the breath and an involuntary murmur throughout the whole Court'. It is needless to summarize the evidence of the fifty-four witnesses examined in support of the indictment. The shamelessness of Probert, the hysteria of his wife, the genuine grief of Richard Weare and of Thomas Thurtell, the ungrammatical officer and constables, the Bonifaces, mellow with their own liquors, the ostlers also somewhat overtaken, except Dick Bingham, who was 'quite undisguised, and seemed to be confident and clear in proportion to the cordials and compounds', and the Court's periodical outbreaks of temper, and the unending struggles of reporters and of the 'fancy' to force their way into coigns of vantage, have been admirably described by eye-witnesses. The two most alert people in Court were the judge and John Thurtell, the latter, as ever, acting a part. 'I should not have omitted to mention,' wrote Herbert, 'an admirable piece of presence of mind and by-play which Thurtell showed towards Clarke, the publican who had been an old acquaintance; on Clarke's turning to bow to him when he entered the witness-box, in which he was about to speak to the prisoner's identity, Thurtell received the bow with a look of ignorant wonder, and elevated his eyebrows as though to say, "How bow to me! I know you not." This could have been but instantaneous, but the intention of the prisoner was evident, and the trick was inimitably well performed.'

In contrast to the theatrical demeanour of Thurtell was the impudently collected manner of the chief witness against him, Probert.

When Probert was called [says Mr Herbert], he was ushered through the dock into the body of the Court. The most intense interest at his entering the witness-box was evidently felt by all persons, in which even the prisoners joined. Hunt stood up and looked much agitated; Thurtell eyed the witness sternly and composedly. Probert was very well dressed, and had a new pair of gloves on.... He did not seem the least ashamed of his situation. ... The face of Probert is marked with deceit in every lineament; the eyes are those of a vicious horse, and the lips are thick and sensual. His forehead recedes villainously in amongst a bush of grizzly black hair, and his ears project out of the like cover.... He stood up against Mr Gurney's exposure with a face of brass. Indeed, he seems to fear nothing but death or bodily pain. His grammar was very nearly as bad as his heart.

The counsel for the defence, able men as they were, could do little to assist their clients. Mr Ward, the surgeon, gave the clearest evidence as to the cause of death, and defied all the efforts of Mr Pitt to entangle him. The evidence of the ostlers and publicans was far stronger than Thurtell had anticipated, and when at a very late hour the Court eventually adjourned he had made up his mind for the worst. It says not a little for his stoutness that next morning 'he looked as though he had passed a good night; and yet he must have been busy in the brain all through the dark hours'. As Probert's face of brass had been the feature of the first day's proceedings, the oration of Thurtell stood out as that of the second.

It would be idle, indeed, and very unfair to the orator, to compare it with the masterpieces of professional advocates. The barrister's life is not at stake. He is performing a duty in which his personal interests are far less closely bound up than are those of a prisoner in person; he has all the advantage of experience and familiarity; he has, nowadays at least, the fullest possible instructions for dealing with the evidence on the other side; he could, in those days, take refuge from the unexplainable facts against the prisoner in the glib pretence that his client's lips were sealed, for at that time the accused was not permitted to give evidence on his own behalf in the witness-box. A man rising to address a jury under such circumstances as Thurtell's was so heavily handicapped that he was not infrequently advised by his counsel to attempt no defence at all. In two previous cases of rape the prisoners had remained mute when called on for their defence, and were acquitted.

The more rhetorical parts of the speech Thurtell had carefully committed to memory; the eloquence was not his own, being a patchwork from the speeches of Charles Phillips and others; its very theatrical manner was wholly in harmony with the character of its author. Its effect is best described in the words of Mr Herbert. 'Thurtell now seemed to retire within himself for half a minute – and then slowly, the crowd being breathlessly silent and anxious – drawing in his breath and gathering up his frame, and looking very steadfastly at the jury, he commenced his defence. He spoke in a deep, measured, and unshaken tone, accompanying it with a rather studied and theatrical action. . . . When he had finished his carefully learnt exordium, and proceeded to deal with the evidence, reading from the notes he had so diligently made, the favourable impression gave way, and before he had finished quoting his long list of alleged wrongful convictions the patience of the audience had been entirely exhausted, and there was so much noise in Court that his powerful tones were well-nigh inaudible.

It is a curious psychological fact that an advocate preaching on the fallibility of circumstantial evidence from the acknowledged blunders of the past nearly always prejudices his own cause. He bores the jury, and leads his hearers to the somewhat illogical conclusion that he must have a very poor case, since he prefers to talk about others. There is no more certain way of irritating a judge or jury than to parade the shade of the late Adolf Beck. Mr Herbert tells us that

this paper was either so ill-written or Thurtell was so indifferent a reader that the effect was quite fatal to the previous flowery appeal to the jury. He stammered, blundered, and seemed confused throughout. . . . When he finished his books and laid aside the paper he seemed to return with joy and strength to his memory, and to muster up all his might for the peroration.

The scene at the close of the speech has never been surpassed for dramatic interest in a Court of justice.

The solid, slow, and appalling tones in which he wrung out these last words can never be imagined by those who were not auditors of it; he worked himself up into a great actor, and his eye for the first time during the trial became alive and eloquent. . . . The final word 'God!' was thrown up with almost gigantic energy, and he stood after its utterance with his arms extended and his face protruded and his chest dilated, as though he dared not move lest he should disturb the still echoing appeal. Such a performance, for a studied performance it surely was, has seldom been seen on the stage, and certainly never off. Thus to act in the very teeth of death demands a nerve which not one man in a thousand ever possessed.

When Hunt was called upon for his defence his feeble voice and shrinking manner were doubly apparent in contrast with the over-wrought energy of his companion. He was entirely unable to read the paper prepared for him, and it was accordingly read by an officer of the Court. When the reading was concluded 'Hunt read a few words of his own on a part of Probert's evidence in a poor, dejected voice, and

53

then leant his head upon his hand. He was evidently wasting away minute by minute. His neckcloth had quite got loose, and his neck looked gaunt and wretched.'

Before Mr Justice Park began to sum up, Thurtell spoke with great firmness to those about him. He said he was sure the judge would take about four hours, but for himself his mind was made up for the worst. Park exhibited his favourable qualities as well as his foibles in the painstaking effort in which he laid the case before the jury. He had displayed throughout the trial minute attention to the matter in hand. Thus we find him recalling Ruthven to prove that Conduit Street was in the parish of St George's, Hanover Square, in the county of Middlesex, and putting the coroner into the box to prove that both Gill's Hill Lane and the pond where the body was found were in Hertfordshire. The object of these questions was to establish the charge precisely as laid in the indictment. Otherwise a counsel of Thesiger's ability might have moved in arrest of judgment that there was no proof of the fact alleged against Hunt that 'With force and arms at the parish of St George's, Hanover Square, etc.,' he counselled, stirred up, and incited his comrade to commit the murder. It may be unnecessary to remark that men's lives often depended in bygone days upon such trifling flaws of form.

The jury took twenty minutes to consider their verdict, and when they returned the foreman was in tears. When the verdict was given 'Thurtell shook not to the last. Hunt was broken down, gone! He sobbed aloud in the wildness of his distress; his faculties seemed thrown down.' Before the *allocutus* or formal calling on the prisoners, which is still part of our immemorial usage in cases of capital conviction, a curious scene occurred, which is thus described in a manuscript of Lord Chelmsford himself :

It was about eight o'clock in the evening of the second day of the trial, when we were all exhausted and in a state of nervous excitement, and the judge was preparing to put on the black cap and pronounce sentence. At this awful moment, Chitty, the celebrated special pleader, rose to move in arrest of judgment. He was always a confused speaker at the best of times, but he was then in such a state of nervous trepidation that he was hardly articulate, and in the midst of a confused jumble of words it was with difficulty that we could understand his objection – that the trial had begun on January the sixth, the feast of the Epiphany, which was a *dies non* like a Sunday, and therefore that the whole proceeding was void. The only answer given by Mr Justice Park was expressed in these terms, 'Why Mr Chitty, the Lord Chief Justice frequently tries causes on Good Friday,' to which Chitty answered, 'Talking of Good Friday puts me in mind of a story,' and then he told the well-known anecdote, but with the omission of Pontius Pilate, the only point.

The motion was overruled, and after a few manly words from John Thurtell asking for a short respite, Sir Alan, labouring under great emotion, passed sentence of death. The theatrical nature of the murderer again asserted itself. Conscious that every eye was upon him while the dreadful words about his body's dissection were falling from the tremulous lips of the venerable judge, he ostentatiously consumed the pinch of snuff which had to that moment been pausing in his fingers.

The respite sought by Thurtell the judge was unable to grant. In all cases of conviction of murder as a principal, death followed judgment with a swiftness that, under the appearance of harshness, was yet the truer mercy. Thurtell occupied the brief remaining hours of life in characteristic fashion. At first the instinctive horror of untimely death unmanned him. When the Rev. Mr Franklin saw him that evening his spirits were completely gone; the reverend gentleman found him sitting in a cell bathed in tears, and evidently oppressed by great mental anguish. He left him in a state of deep dejection. His natural courage soon, however, enabled him to face the inevitable end. He was generally considered to have shown genuine contrition and to have revealed unsuspected depths of goodness. The gaolers said that he was a kind, good-hearted fellow, so obliging and friendly that they never had a prisoner whom they so much regretted. And such seems to have been his general character, when not inflamed at once by the desire for revenge and of game. The fair sex, in particular, commiserated his fate, but a misplaced sympathy was well-nigh universal.

In anticipation of a record demand Jemmy Catnach prepared a series of execution broadsides. He is stated to have reaped £500 in pennies from the crime. It has even been stated that the word 'catch-penny' owes its origin to a trick he played upon the public shortly after the stroke of justice had fallen upon the murderer, in bringing out a print headed 'Weare Alive Again' – explaining to deluded purchasers that by a typographical error no space had been left after 'We'.

Enormous crowds flocked down from town to see the hero of the hour turned off. A stream of smart vehicles blocked the roads to Hertford on the night of Thursday, 8 January. Many elegantly attired females were noticed among those who drove down, and a heated controversy was maintained in the Press as to whether these were but Cyprians, or represented the social world as well. Meantime the bards of England were busy with their ballads. One wrote as follows:

> The helpless man sprung [sic] from the gig
> And strove the road to gain,
> But Thurtell pounced on him and dashed
> His pistol through his brain,
> Then drawing forth his murderous knife
> As over him he stood,
> He cut his throat, and, tiger-like,
> Did drink his reeking blood.

And another minstrel:

> They knocked him down
> With a pocket pistol,
> His throat they badly cut,
> Then into a ditch
> In a sack well stich [sic]
> This wounded man they put.

Meantime Thurtell spent his time in typical murderer fashion – in forgiving the world for the injuries it had done him, in evading questions touching his guilt, in somewhat morbid religious exercises, and in occasional outbreaks of the real man, 'Bloody, bold, and resolute', threatening vengeance on those who had betrayed him. The insincerity of his repentance is shown by nothing more clearly than by his parting words with Hunt, when he again reproached that wretched man for his disclosures, without which there could have been no conviction, and by his solicitude that his oration should appear correctly in the public prints. 'The cold-blooded murderer,' observed the late Dr Benjamin Howard, 'feels no remorse other than the chagrin at the mistake in not securing immunity.'

The scene at the execution itself was copiously described in the newspapers of the day. It was marked by all those disorderly circumstances and mishaps which invariably attended the gathering together of huge crowds of dissolute and dangerous persons. The professional pillagers were present in force. The prisoner's friends gathered at the foot of the scaffold. Egan was there. The infamous Probert, who after his exposure had proceeded with unblushing front to a tavern, where he fell to upon a bottle of wine, had wished to be present also, but the Rev. Mr Lloyd urged upon him the propriety of a return to town, and he was actually proceeding to take his seat in the public stage when the worthy pastor pressed upon him some money for a chaise. Thurtell died firmly. The gallows was the first of its sort erected in Hertford. It launched its victim into eternity with convenient speed. A loud report was heard, says *The Times*, at the moment when the neck was dislocated by the fall. Borrow in later years was wont to say that it was a shame to have hanged such a man. 'Why, when his neck broke, it went off like a pistol.'

Other accounts say that the dying man was heard to give a deep groan. Just before the drop fell he had been observed to bow to someone in the crowd. Egan took the compliment for himself. Borrow tells us that his last recognition was intended for a humble friend, who had driven a great distance to take his leave 'of the only friend I had in the world'.

'We could perceive,' said *The Medical Adviser* (17 January 1824), 'in his countenance, when he was on the fatal platform, that the feeling of irritation was working in his breast.' A curious incident was noticed by *The Times* reporter and others. 'Four messengers, with the fleetest horses, were dispatched from Hertford to town the moment the fall of the drop had for ever closed this source of disquietude.' It was suggested that these horse expresses conveyed to Lemon and other criminal associates of the dead man that he had died without making any disclosure. But it is difficult to see how the messengers could have had any knowledge as to what passed between the doomed man and his gaolers. It is far more probable that the expresses were bound with copy for Fleet Street, since at that early period of journalism occurrences were described by persons who had actually seen them, and thus there were no chronicles of events which never happened.

The corpse was conveyed in a gig to St Bartholomew's Hospital for dissection – he could not, even in death, be divided from such a vehicle. A finger was cut from the hand on the journey to town in order to provide, some said, a tobacco stopper, or more probably through the superstitious belief in the touch of a hanged man's hand as a cure for wens. At the hospital vast crowds swarmed to see the body. A pretence was made of limiting the admissions to the Faculty, but imposters, by the easy affirmative reply to the question whether they could answer any conundrum in anatomy, had no difficulty in getting in. For some weeks the famous Abernethy publicly dissected the body. By the time he had concluded, the corpse had begun to be offensive. Nevertheless, thousands visited its ghastly lying-in-state. Daily descriptions whetted the morbid appetite of the public. Phrenologists and physiognomists squabbled over the character of the departed – as if it had not already been sufficiently laid bare. The former professed to discover benevolent qualities in excess; benevolence itself was thirteen, combativeness 'very slight – only six', and destructiveness was almost non-existent – a paltry five. Such rubbish misled the Primate of Ireland, the acute Dr Whately, into forming an estimate of the dead man which does little credit to his understanding in such matters.

The physiognomists were happier.

If phrenology did not prove him a murderer, physiognomy did. The narrow forehead, thick eyebrows, small eyes with fat swellings under them, long jaws, curled nostrils, thick lips with the under one falling, thin hair and circumscribed beard, the lines of the cheeks and the angles of the lips almost continuous – all develop the temper and disposition of the criminal far more intelligibly than the present system of phrenology. (*Medical Adviser*, 17 and 24 January 1824.)

Meantime, on the eve of his execution, Hunt was reprieved and sent to the *Justitia* hulk, preparatory to transportation. The Home Office Records show that he arrived at the hulk at Portsmouth late on 28 January 1824. His utter vileness is strikingly illustrated by an anecdote in *The Times* of 24 February 1824. He actually sang in the chapel the song he had sung to Mrs Probert after the murder – the duet 'All's Well'. To some casual visitors he remarked, 'Jack has silenced many a man. Why, he disposed of three or four in the house at Manchester Buildings.' In a confession, authenticated by Mr Clutterbuck, the Justice, and embodied with all its faults of grammar and spelling in the report of Mr Jones the justices' clerk, Hunt repeated these wild charges. A Mr Cotton and others who had unaccountably disappeared were supposed to have been made away with by this gang. It is useless to speculate upon the truth of Hunt's insinuations. He seems to have taken a perverted pride in being taken for a 'Turpin lad' instead of the craven coward he was. Thurtell was such a clumsy murderer that Weare's was probably a first attempt. Hunt was placed on board the *Countess of*

Harecourt, a convict ship, on 8 March. She sailed on the 16th, and Hunt, instead of being murdered on the voyage, as Ballantine has related, duly landed in Botany Bay, was moved inland to 'The Felons' Paradise' in Wellington Valley, and later on was assigned as a servant to a Mr Jonathan Slattery at Bathurst.

Mr Barber Beaumont continued to pursue his proceedings in the matter of Thomas Thurtell's claim against his office. On 11 February 1924, Mr Serjeant Taddy moved for a rule absolute for a new trial of the action heard the previous June, but the Court, through Lord Chief Justice Gifford, refused the rule. On Thursday, 3 June, the proceedings initiated before the murder against both the Thurtells and Borthwick, the porter at Watling Street, and Snowden, who had acted as agent for the Thurtells in the re-sales to Margrave of the goods purchased from Todd, Morrison, and the others, came up in the King's Bench before Lord Chief Justice Abbot and a special jury, in the form of a trial for conspiracy to defraud the County Fire Office. The nature of the evidence in support of the charge has already been indicated. After some spirited advocacy on both sides, the Court, in a luminous summing-up, pointed out that the issue was not whether the fire was accidental or felonious, although that had a material bearing on the case, but whether the accused man had fraudulently conspired to claim in respect of goods not on the premises at the time, and so not destroyed by the perils insured against. In the end Thomas Thurtell and Snowden were convicted, and Borthwick was acquitted. Sentence of two years' imprisonment was passed, and the prisoners were moved to Newgate.

Probert, who had withdrawn from Hertford amid the execrations of the entire populace (after a characteristic piece of meanness in trying to evade payment of a small debt due to the turnkeys), came up to London, and, with his usual matchless impudence, wrote to *The Times* and other leading papers threatening to issue writs for libel on his character. A shady attorney named Jacob Mann also wrote to Messrs

Knight & Lacy, publishers, demanding to know the name of their solicitors, as Probert intended to take instant proceedings against them for publishing Pierce Egan's *Recollections of John Thurtell*. His threats were treated with contempt, and, in utter poverty, he was driven as an outcast from place to place. Taking refuge with a farmer named Meredith, he repaid his benefactor by stealing his mare, valued at £5. He came to London once more, and disposed of her for a small sum. He was soon apprehended, and tried at the April sessions at the Old Bailey in 1825. A feeble effort was made by his counsel in cross-examination of the prosecutor's wife to suggest that she might have lent the mare. This she denied, but had Probert appeared to be a bailer he must have been acquitted at common law, though he had sold the animal. The prisoner was genteelly dressed in black, and exhibited not the least appearance of fear. He read his address with great composure; it amounted to no more than a plea *ad misericordiam*, the wretch not denying his offence, and, after a few words from Lord Chief Justice Abbot, the jury found him guilty, and he received sentence of death. Confidently relying on the Royal Mercy, he left the dock undismayed.

As if the fate of his companion had not made the phrenologists look sufficiently foolish, a crazy professor of the science wrote to Probert in prison just before his trial suggesting that he would certainly escape by contending that a man with a head like his was an inevitable criminal. This deterministic argument did not commend itself to the prisoner's good sense.

No respite arrived, and on Sunday, 19 June, Probert took a last leave of his wife and mother, and, after the horrible customs of the times, listened to the condemned sermon.

Probert's wife and mother did not bid him a final farewell till yesterday afternoon. The wife appeared to be bereft of her reason. The wretched man, who had been clinging pertinaciously to life to the last, is said in the course of the evening to have discovered some disposition to the admonitions of the Reverend Ordinary [Dr

Cotton]. .... It has been intimated that Probert wrote some time back to the Earl of Uxbridge.

At the condemned sermon

his appearance was just such as might have been expected by those who read the accounts in general circulation about him. He walked with a firm step to the pew appointed for those who are irrevocably doomed to death. He sat down, put his hands to his face, and seemed to be quite overpowered with anguish. Probert exhibits one strong evidence of 'a mind diseased'. His hair, which was quite dark when he appeared with his brother murderer at Hertford, is now almost completely grey. Calamity and crime have changed it. ... Thomas Thurtell, who is still confined in Newgate, was not at the chapel.

When informed of his fate, 'his limbs shook, and when he could distinctly speak he said, "Oh, God, is this the way I am to do, or die? Oh, it is not for this I die." All attempts to recover him from his fears and horrors were useless.' At the place of execution 'his limbs were completely palsied, and his agitation dreadful'. He died on 20 June, in his thirty-seventh year, and was buried in the presence of enormous throngs on the 22nd in St Martin's churchyard. He, too, has won, like Thurtell, an imperishable distinction; the *Morning Chronicle*, by associating his gig with his apparent gentility, provided a definition of 'gentleman' which will last as long as our language, and led Carlyle to coin his familiar 'Gigmania' and 'Gigmanity', and George Eliot to speak of 'proud respectability in a gig'.

Yet not with his death was the tragedy of Gill's Hill forgotten. Nothing is more curious than the fascination these truculent ruffians excited in men of genius and learning. Scott, proceeding north on 28 May 1828, 'could not resist going out of his way to see the spot where William Weare, who "dwelt in Lyon's Inn", was murdered', and has sketched in a few masterly words the weird appearance of the cottage, which long continued to be a place of pilgrimage, until it was finally demolished about 1888.

Literary and artistic genius were alike attracted by the

crime. That the rag-tag and bobtail should have revelled in the chapbooks and ballads is in no way surprising. It was just such a murder as the proletariat would appreciate; the desperate and short-sighted wickedness of it might not disgust the rabble. What perplexes is that men of great refinement felt the charm as well. Was it that the story revealed an altogether lower depth of merely sordid criminality than had ever been sounded before? Was it the contrast between the nadir of moral degradation attained by the assassin and the zenith of respectability of some of his relations? Was it the theatrical and meretricious quality of the defence? Whatever the cause or combination of causes, this murder, in which guilt was so transparent and the romantic element so lacking, excited England not only more than any other single crime up to then, but more, if we can judge by the columns devoted to it, than some of the great events of history which occurred about that time. Weare's funeral was described at far more length than the illustrious Erskine's which happened during the fever of excitement the Gill's Hill story had called forth.

To the criminologist of today, the murder is not very absorbing. The personalities of the criminals contained nothing psychologically puzzling. The murderer himself was just one of those favourite sons of a doting mother whose early faults condoned have carried them with ever-hastening feet along the primrose path. He displayed occasionally those superficially amiable qualities which, at least in doubtful company, may win a bastard popularity and sometimes earn the title of a good fellow for the least estimable of men. Like many another whose means of livelihood are criminal or fraudulent, he was free with money – when he had it. Nothing more conclusively demonstrates the criminal character of Thurtell than his passion for notoriety. Incapable of achieving honourable fame, he did not blush to be numbered among the Newgate Calendar heroes.

Excuses have been made for Thurtell on the score of supposed injuries received by him at Weare's hands. Such will not bear critical scrutiny. The murderer had no doubt to buy his experience when he first began to frequent gambling hells. But this was some years before the murder. He had been intimate with his victim throughout, and by continuing to associate with him plainly showed that, though he might have been a pigeon at first, he was afterwards a co-adventurer in villainy. He was perfectly aware that Weare was likely to have £2,000 or thereabouts on his person, and no one who reads the various law proceedings can fail to be persuaded that John Thurtell stood in October 1823 in imperative need of a large sum of money, just as Palmer did when he killed Cooke; and Weare was selected, not in revenge for injuries, but because he was known to carry the 'blunt' on his person. As to the division of the spoils, who can doubt that, as Sir Walter put it, the murderer 'bucketed his pals'? He had admittedly searched the body before Probert and Hunt came up, and had taken the watch and the purse. When he again searched it, he produced the pocket-book containing three five-pound notes, saying, 'This is all he has got.' Is it not most palpable that he had left those notes there as a blind when he rifled the body of the money.

Yet, for all its commonplace ruffianism, the Gill's Hill murder is not completely without interest for the student of today. The picture of life and manners now more than a century ago – the brutality of the prize ring, the free libation to Bacchus (even the witnesses being mostly intoxicated), the cumbrous and antiquated legal procedure, the 'horse expresses' upon which a greedy public was dependent for its daily budget of horror, the broadsides, and the ghastly publicity of the execution and dissection – how strikingly does all this bring out what is meant by a century of progress. What a different England was that of George IV from the England of today!

Frederick Nodder

· 1937 ·

BY

WINIFRED DUKE

ABOUT four o'clock on 5 January 1937, Miss Daisy Hawley, a teacher at the Wesleyan School, Guildhall Street, Newark, saw her scholars depart after the day's labours. Presumably they clattered out, glad, as children will be, to escape from the confinement of the class-room into the open air. One child was destined never to attend school again. It was the last time that Miss Hawley saw this pupil alive.

Mona Lilian Tinsley, the child in question, was just ten years old, having been born on 14 November 1926. She lived with her parents, respectable working-class folk, at No. 11 Thoresby Avenue, a small house on a corporation estate. Her father was a coal carter. Mona was one of a family of seven boys and girls. Her teacher described her as an intelligent and bright little girl. On 5 January, a Tuesday, she had gone as usual to morning school, returning for her mid-day dinner at home. Mona came back to attend the afternoon session, leaving with the rest of the pupils at four o'clock. She was dressed in a light-blue jumper-suit, a double-breasted brown tweed coat, and Wellington boots, but wore no hat. Thoresby Avenue was some twenty minutes' walk from Guildhall Street, and normally Mona should have reappeared at No. 11 by half past four. When she did not, her father and mother apparently felt no anxiety regarding her, although it was a January night, cold, dark, and disagreeable. Not until seven o'clock did they institute inquiries as to her whereabouts.

Mr Tinsley had relations in the district, but these, when

approached, knew nothing of Mona. The immediate neighbours were not told that she was missing, a regrettable happening in the light of subsequent events, as two of them, a Mrs Hird who lived at 15 Thoresby Avenue, and a schoolboy whose home was next door to the Tinsleys, afterwards came forward with information of material importance. Between 9.30 and 9.45 p.m. Mr Tinsley went to the police and reported his little girl's disappearance.

Here it may not be out of place to give some description of Newark and the surrounding district. The town itself, a busy manufacturing one of roughly 20,000 inhabitants, lies in the Midlands. Its chief claim to historical distinction consists of the fact that King John, of evil memory, breathed his last in Newark Castle, the remains of which can still be seen above the brawling of the Trent. Newark stands on the Great North Road, on the eastern boundary of Nottinghamshire, within a few miles of the Lincolnshire border. The Chesterfield Canal and several local rivers – the Trent, the Idle, the Ryton – all figured in the story, as did the more distant towns of Retford and Sheffield. Out of the latter emerged the enigmatic figure of Frederick Nodder.

Nodder the individual remains a complete puzzle. At neither of his trials did anything transpire which revealed who he really was, what were his antecedents, where he came from prior to his fateful introduction into the Tinsley household, by what means he supported himself, why he passed under an assumed name, and whether he had any relatives or connexions. In the month of October 1935, a man in his early forties, calling himself Frederick Hudson, although his real name was Frederick Nodder, arrived to lodge with Mr and Mrs Tinsley. The latter had three sisters and a brother, all married people, who lived in Sheffield. One of the sisters, Mrs Grimes, introduced Hudson as a friend of herself and her husband. The new lodger remained for about three weeks and became 'Uncle Fred' to the young Tinsleys. During his second trial the accused stated that while lodging with the Tinsleys he had continued on the best of terms with the family. He left because of some difficulty in paying his rent, an assertion corroborated by Mr Tinsley, who added that otherwise there had been no unpleasantness between himself and the self-styled Hudson. At no time did Mona's father give the lodger any authority to remove her from her home or parents.

Under the supervision of Mr Barnes, the Chief Constable of Newark Borough Police Force, steps were immediately taken to trace Mona Tinsley. All schools in Newark had long been shut for the day, and the pupils in bed by the time the police were made aware of Mona's disappearance, but throughout the cold January night the authorities pursued their inquiries. Certain derelict property in the town and the banks of the Trent were exhaustively searched, while, acting on the supposition that the child might have been conveyed away in a lorry, the heavy motor traffic on the Great North Road was carefully checked. Early next morning the principals of local schools were asked that directly their pupils assembled Mona's disappearance should be intimated to them, and any child who had seen her on the previous day after 4 p.m. was to be ready to communicate particulars to the police. Innumerable children thought or imagined or believed that they had seen Mona, and every separate statement required investigating. The most valuable one came from William Henry Plackett, an eleven-year-old schoolboy, a pupil of a school in Appleton Gate Street, Newark. This boy lived at No. 13 Thoresby Avenue, and knew Mona and her family as neighbours On the crucial date, between half past four and a quarter to five, he saw her 'near the bus station opposite where the buses start'. There was a man with her, 'facing her, about a yard off'. Plackett's description of the man was vague, but he thought that he would know him again.

The whole day (6 January) the police worked ceaselessly, certain officers making inquiries around the town, and others discovering and questioning the drivers and conductors of vehicles on the local bus services. Later, two women were interviewed. One had noticed Mona the previous afternoon near the station from which the hourly bus to Retford started, and the other was the previously mentioned Mrs Hird. Between a quarter to four and four o'clock (she fixed the time by having gone to fetch her little girl from school) while walking down Balderton Street, she saw a man standing against the door of St Mary's School at the end of Guildhall Street. He was alone, and she described him as 'looking towards the Wesleyan School door. He was just looking to see if he could see anyone.' She recognized him as the Tinsley's former lodger. 'He used to live next door but one to where I lived,' and she knew him quite well. They did not speak. Armed with this slender clue Mr Barnes went to have a further interview with Mr and Mrs Tinsley. Both proved extremely reticent about their former non-paying guest. When asked casually if she had ever had a lodger, Mrs Tinsley instantly rejoined : 'Oh, it couldn't be him.' A certain amount of pressure at length elicited the fact that about fifteen months earlier Hudson had stayed with the Tinsleys, but all that Mrs Tinsley knew was that her sister knew him. She herself was unaware of his real name.

Assiduous inquiries around Newark resulted in the tracing by the late afternoon of 6 January of Charles Edward Reville, a bus driver for the Lincolnshire Roadcar Company. On 5 January he had been in charge of the 4.45 bus from Newark to Retford, a distance of some twenty-two miles. He also acted as conductor, and noticed a child, wearing a brown coat, and hatless, who boarded the bus about five minutes' walk from the Wesleyan School in Guildhall Street. A man was with her. He tendered the conductor a half-crown return ticket for himself and bought a single half fare, costing tenpence, for the little girl. The two alighted at Grove Street, Retford. Reville's information was not available until after Mrs Tinsley's Sheffield relatives had been interviewed. These people were vaguely aware that Mrs Grimes was on friendly terms with someone called 'Fred', but professed ignorance of his surname or address. Mrs

Grimes and her husband were next seen at their house, No. 9 Neil Road, Sheffield. Both denied knowing anybody styled 'Hudson', but in the course of the interview Mr Grimes mentioned the name 'Nodder', and this inadvertent admission was of considerable importance. The couple alike averred that they had not seen this individual for some length of time, and Mrs Grimes maintained that she did not know where he lived. As it was subsequently brought out that she had been in the habit of visiting him regularly and had telephoned to him the day before, the statement was rather strange. Investigations into the records at Sheffield Police Station followed, and a warrant was discovered for the non-payment of a sum of eighteen pounds, arrears accumulated under an affiliation order against a Frederick Nodder. It now transpired that Nodder – or Hudson – was a married man, separated from his wife, a respectable, hard-working woman with two children, who had suffered much through her husband's infidelities. Nodder possessed abilities as a motor-driver and mechanic, and had been at one time in good private service, but lost this employment because of his intemperate habits and dishonesty. During the First World War he served in the R.A.M.C. The breaking-up of his married life followed a Court order obliging him to pay for the maintenance of an illegitimate child of which he was the father. Nodder was then living in Sheffield, but in consequence of the bastardy proceedings against him found it prudent to change his name and shift his camp. Soon after leaving his wife Nodder met Grimes, who gave him access to his house. Despite an unpleasing exterior and his revolting personal habits, Nodder appears to have had a certain attraction for his acquaintances. He persuaded Mr Grimes to buy a second-hand car and used to drive the couple about in it. More than once an expedition was made to Mrs Grimes's sister and brother-in-law at Newark, Nodder being introduced to the Tinsleys by his assumed name of Hudson. After leaving them he took up his abode in a small house in Retford, where Mrs Grimes began to visit him every week.

In June 1936, Nodder went to live at Peacehaven, one of four semi-detached houses of the village called Hayton. Hayton lies three and a half miles from Retford, connected with it by a bus service running from Gainsborough in Lincolnshire, through Clarborough village to Retford, thence to Worksop, and eventually to Sheffield. At Hayton Nodder obtained work with a haulage contractor, but once more drink was the cause of his losing this employment.

The police had a second interview with Mrs Grimes, no more productive of information than the first. While she was being interrogated other officials questioned a neighbour, an old man, who told them that on 27 December he had noticed a lorry parked near the Grimes's house, and he remembered the word 'Retford' painted on it. Mrs Grimes stated that she knew nothing of this vehicle. In a further interview with her husband he admitted that Nodder had called on him about Christmas, but he still denied all knowledge of Nodder's whereabouts. Investigations at licensed premises and garages in Retford shortly established the fact that a man of the name Nodder lived at Hayton. The Chief Constable and his subordinates at once went there, arriving approximately about seven o'clock at night.

Smeath Road, a lonely road, on which stood Peacehaven and its adjoining houses, leads from Clarborough, a neighbouring village, and links with another road running from Retford to the hamlet of Tiln. On the way, a mile and a half from Nodder's house, lies a place named Bolham Shuttle, adjacent to which was a tannery. The River Idle, normally a sluggish stream of water, full of deep holes, flows through Retford to Bawtry, passing Bolham Shuttle. At Tiln the road ends in the Idle, rather more than two miles from Peacehaven. The Chesterfield Canal runs within fifty yards of the northern side of the house. The garden of Peacehaven led on to a wide ploughed field and ultimately to a churchyard. At the time the road was unlighted and the property on it recently built.

Nodder's next-door neighbour was a Mrs Simpson, her

house being the first on the left, and Nodder's the second. Peacehaven had no telephone, so she allowed him to use hers, and she also received any telephone messages for him. On the morning of 5 January a call from Sheffield came at 9 a.m. Mrs Simpson summoned Nodder to take it, but did not know what was said. She happened not to see him again that day, but the following morning (Wednesday, 6 January) she was in her back-garden about 9.30, and had some conversation with him over the wall. He asked to borrow a gardener's fork and spade, both of which Mrs Simpson lent him. Later she noticed Nodder working in his garden. During the forenoon she was indoors, but about midday, on leaving her house, saw Nodder still gardening. They 'had a chat', Nodder's garden being the topic. There was no mention of a child, or any reference to Mrs Simpson's own little girl. At about a quarter past three, from a window of her house, Mrs Simpson observed Nodder coming from his back-garden towards his house. When Mrs Simpson went out at five o'clock she noted that the electric light was on in Nodder's kitchen. The door of the kitchen stood open. An hour later she left her house once more and the light was no longer burning.

Next door but one to Peacehaven was a house called Endeavour, occupied by a Miss Whittaker. She employed as a daily maid Doreen Jessie Jarman, whose hours for working were from 8 a.m. till twelve. On 6 January this girl, happening to go to the dust-bin, from which was afforded a favourable view of the back door of Peacehaven, noticed that the door was open, and a little girl was standing in the aperture. She appeared to be eight or nine years of age. (Mona Tinsley was very small for a girl of ten.) The child wore, Miss Jarman thought, a pale-blue dress. Nodder was digging in his garden. The maid fixed the time – twelve o'clock – because it was just about the hour when she finished her work and went to her home in Church Lane, Clarborough – a distance of a mile and a half. She was positive that it could not have been more than ten minutes past twelve at the latest, and refused to alter her opinion at the trial, despite counsel's questions and suggestions.

When the police arrived at Peacehaven the place was in darkness. Inquiries instituted amongst the immediate neighbours revealed that Nodder had been seen during the day, but no child was either seen or heard. (Miss Jarman's evidence did not become available until later.) Mr Barnes left an officer at the house and went away himself, returning again. In his own words : 'It was a dark night, and it was a rough night. By that I mean there was half a gale of wind blowing.' The Chief Constable stationed a county policeman at the Clarborough end of Smeath Road, and, with the car driver and the detective-sergeant who had accompanied him from Sheffield, took up his position on the unlighted road opposite to the gate leading to Mrs Simpson's house. They had a long, grim, cold vigil. Eventually, at eleven o'clock, through the blackness and the rush of wind, the watchers heard footsteps coming from the direction of Retford across the Chesterfield Canal. 'A figure loomed up out of the darkness right on me.' Nodder – for it was he – seeing a light in Mrs Simpson's house, and a car standing before the door, accosted the Chief Constable, inquiring if anybody was ill. Mr Barnes replied that he did not know and asked why Nodder was interested. Nodder explained that he lived next door and agreed to the Chief Constable's suggestion that they should go into the house as Mr Barnes wanted to see him. The whole party entered together by the back door. Here Mr Barnes noticed a curious little incident. As he and Nodder approached the rear of the house along a gravel path Nodder walked on tip-toe. Why? Was he about to enter a dwelling which had been the scene of recent death? Inside, with the electric light turned on, Nodder was found to be wearing a blue overcoat, an old navy-blue suit, and a brown cap. His brown shoes were not muddy.

Mr Barnes told Nodder who he was. Nodder did not appear to him to be surprised, or even taken aback. The Chief Constable then produced the bastardy warrant. Nodder acknowledged his identity and admitted that the document referred to him. Mr Barnes then explained that he was making inquiries into Mona Tinsley's disappearance, to which Nodder rejoined, 'I know nothing about it.' A photograph of Mona, supplied by her father, was shown to Nodder, and he was asked if would like to account for his movements the previous day. Nodder made a short statement, not interrupted in any way, which the Chief Constable took down in his note-book. He read this over to Nodder, who signed it. The statement was as follows :

I went from Retford to Carlton on the 11.20 bus by myself, and from there I went to Newark. I caught the 3.45 p.m. bus from Newark and came home. When I got on the bus I took a ticket to Newark with the intention of getting off at Carlton. I saw a man at Newark who works for Teal's on a barge. I spoke to him about prospects, and he gave me Mr Teal's address. I believe I wore my sand-coloured trousers on Sunday last. The photograph is that of a niece of a friend of mine in Sheffield. I have not seen her for fifteen months.

The police party remained in the house for about forty minutes. Nodder stayed in the kitchen with two officers while the Chief Constable explored Peacehaven. Downstairs there were two rooms, a living-room and a kitchen, and upstairs two bedrooms and a bathroom. The only bed was in a largish room at the back above the kitchen and overlooking the garden. (One of the minor mysteries of the case is how Nodder, even before the present acute housing shortage, managed to rent or buy a house of this size.) It had been scantily furnished on the hire-purchase system. No trace could be found of any child's recent presence, but articles of clothing were discovered answering to the description of the attire worn by the man seen at the bus-stop in Newark the previous day.

Peacehaven was locked up and Nodder removed in custody to Newark. The police were strongly of the opinion that the case might develop into one of murder, and spared no pains to find evidence in support of this theory. The committal order enabled the authorities to hold Nodder on the relatively trivial charge of non-payment, while seeking to discover either Mona Tinsley or her dead body, when a much more serious accusation would be brought against him. A thorough search of Nodder's house was made next day (7 January). It was indescribably dirty, and the bed-clothes and bedding of the double bed were likewise filthy. The bed bore signs of having been slept in, and beneath one of the pillows two soiled handkerchiefs were found, together with a packet of sweets and a tin of vaseline. The floor-boards were removed and the inside of the house investigated, but nothing bearing on the case was found. An examination at the Forensic Laboratory of Nodder's garments and the bed-linen and bedding brought no helpful results. Nodder's recent horticultural activities were suspect, and the entire garden of Peacehaven was dug up. One spot held a sinister suggestion of a possible grave, and a well was discovered, but no trace of Mona Tinsley appeared. A search through newspapers and magazines in the house revealed a piece of paper scribbled over with childish handwriting. Similar paper was likewise found, as well as the journal from which the extract had been copied. This handwriting was afterwards identified as Mona Tinsley's. Plates, washed but not dried, were on a draining-board. One of them carried a child's fingerprint, but it was impossible to connect this with comparable fingerprints on Mona Tinsley's possessions such as toys or books.

The same day (7 January) an identification parade was held at Newark Police Station. Seven witnesses, including the boy Plackett, Mrs Hird, and the other woman, were asked if they could pick out Nodder. Four of them failed to do so. The remaining three were convinced that he was the man they had seen with Mona Tinsley. Plackett recognized him as a man he remembered lodging at Mrs Tinsley's house 'a nice long time ago', who had been styled 'Uncle Fred' by the children. Reville, the bus-conductor, was certain that Nodder, accompanied by a little girl, had alighted from his vehicle in Retford, but Nodder persistently denied having

travelled on it that day. The police, realizing that they had
not made much progress in their search for Mona Tinsley,
arranged for a message to be broadcast on the National
Wavelength regarding her disappearance, and the Press was
asked to cooperate. Informations were issued to the Police
Gazette and West Riding Reports, as well as to all police
stations. Additionally posters were circulated, bearing the
missing child's photograph and description.

The first result of these measures appeared when Mr
Stanley George Betts, a motor-engineer, living at 32 Chapel
Gate, Retford, came forward. He stated that on 5 January
he had been a passenger on Reville's bus, which he boarded
at Tuxford at 5.30, arriving at Retford about six o'clock.
Amongst his fellow-passengers he noted and remembered a
man and a young girl. The latter appeared to him to be
probably nine years of age. Mr Betts attended an identification parade at which he picked out Nodder as the child's
companion on this journey.

Two other men, Charles Ernest Whitlam and Harry
Cordell, labourers, who were both acquaintances of Nodder, had chanced to be standing in Cannon Square, Retford
about 6.45 on the evening of 5 January. These stated that
they saw Nodder come from the bus stand 'across to Church
gate', in the direction of Hayton. A small child followed him.
She ran towards him, according to Whitlam, 'after him, like'.
The child was 'facing the Church', and Whitlam was unable to say whether it was a girl. He spoke to Nodder when
the latter was five or six yards away, 'shouted to him', but
Nodder failed to answer. Whitlam was annoyed and 'never
took any more particular notice of him; I never bothered'.
It was ten months since Whitlam had last seen Nodder – in
a public house, in March 1936. Whitlam did not know where
Nodder lived and thought that the child was his own. The
spot, it appeared, was two to two and a half miles' distance
from Peacehaven. Nodder's presence and that of the little
girl was corroborated by Whitlam's companion Cordell.

On 8 January, Police-Constable G. E. Coe was on duty

at the police office and at ten o'clock at night saw Nodder in his cell. Nodder asked the constable to get in touch with a detective-sergeant as he wished to make a statement. Detective-Sergeant Francis was informed and interviewed Nodder some ten minutes later. Nodder said, 'If you will get Mrs Grimes over from Sheffield I will make a statement which will lead to the recovery of Mona Tinsley alive and well.' The following day (9th) in the Chief Constable's office Nodder was confronted with Mona's aunt. He greeted her with, 'These chaps know all about us.' Then he asked her, 'Have you seen Mona? Is Mona at your house?' Mrs Grimes replied in the negative to both questions. Nodder's next words, still addressed to her, were, 'Then I am responsible.' He turned to the Chief Constable, saying, 'You had better take a statement.' After he had been cautioned, the statement Nodder made was taken by Mr Barnes and read over to Nodder, who signed it on each page and at the end. It ran thus :

I have been cautioned and told that I am not obliged to say anything, but that whatever I say will be taken down in writing and may be used in evidence. Whatever I tell you now is going to be right. You have got my movements up to the time I saw the man at the wharf, and that is correct. Well, after that I walked about, and in London Road I met Mona who spoke to me. She saw me first. She asked how auntie and Peter was so I asked her if she would like to see auntie, and she asked me if I would take her to see auntie, particularly Peter. [Peter was Mona Tinsley's cousin, and the baby boy of Mrs Grimes.]
She had never seen him. I explained to her that she would not be able to see auntie and Peter till next day. She said she wanted to come with me, and, foolishly, I agreed, repenting my action as soon as I started off. Expecting to see Mrs Grimes the following day and then finding out I should not, I realized my best plan would be to send her to Neil Road with a letter explaining my actions fully, and on Wednesday night I took her on the 6.45 bus from Retford to Worksop, giving her fullest instructions how to get to Neil Road both verbally and on paper. I then returned to Retford from Worksop by bus. I believe it was the quarter past

eight bus out of Worksop, arriving in Retford at a quarter to nine. I called at the Criterion, had a drink, arrived at the Sherwood Foresters' Arms, Moorgate, arriving there at nine, left at ten, walked home by Tiln Lane walking. Then I spoke to you outside Simpson's. With the letter I gave her I explained all my actions, and asked Mrs Grimes's advice. I do not think there is anything else I can add to that.

It is obvious that certain parts of Nodder's statement were true, but the story of his having dispatched Mona Tinsley, alone, to Sheffield, late in the evening, sounded highly improbable and unconvincing. From Nodder's house to Retford the distance was at least three miles, from Retford to Worksop eight miles, from Worksop to Sheffield nineteen miles, and the whole journey from Retford to Sheffield twenty-seven or eight. To reach Neil Road, where Mrs Grimes lived, necessitated walking from the bus terminus at Sheffield along one street to the tram, and then taking a twopenny tram ride. No. 9 was right at the other end of Neil Road. It should be remembered that it was a dark winter night, blustery and disagreeable, and Mona had not visited her aunt, the latter stated, for several years. As Nodder had gone to Sheffield to see Grimes just after Christmas, his subsequent explanation that he had not accompanied Mona because he was afraid to be seen in the town owing to the bastardy warrant against him scarcely has the ring of truth.

At Nodder's first trial, Mrs Grimes stated in the course of her evidence that Mona was her niece, with whom she was on affectionate terms, but she had not seen her for sixteen months. Mona had come to Neil Road with her mother, 'a considerable time ago', when she was quite a small child. Mrs Grimes had no knowledge of her whereabouts. Nodder she had known for about four years. She was in the habit of visiting him at Peacehaven regularly, Thursdays being the day she usually went. At 9 a.m. on 5 January she telephoned to him from a Sheffield call-box, by way of Mrs Simpson's telephone, to say that she could not come over. The conversation was to stress this, and mainly concerned haulage work, 'what he was after'. Pressed by Mr Norman Birkett, the prosecuting counsel, Mrs Grimes acknowleged that Nodder expected a visit from her, probably on the Thursday, as she had visited him on Saturday, 2 January, and then arranged to go to Peacehaven the following week on the 7th. She stated that she wrote and posted a letter to him on the evening of the 5th, its contents corroborating what she had said over the telephone as to her inability to come to Nodder's house next day but one. Mrs Grimes proved a most unsatisfactory witness. She hedged and hesitated under examination and cross-examination; her replies to most queries or suggestions being 'I do not know, I am sure.'

The next day (10 January) at a quarter to six in the evening, the Chief Constable charged Nodder with 'the whole of Section 56 of the Offences against the Person Act'. This, reduced to simpler terms, meant a charge of taking the child Mona Tinsley away from her home by force or fraud. Nodder replied that he had not taken her by force.

The police, acting on Nodder's statement, concentrated especially on the 6.45 p.m. bus from Worksop to Sheffield, and a message was broadcast asking that any person who had travelled by this vehicle on that particular night should come forward. Philip Percival Levick, a conductor employed by the Sheffield Transport Board, was interviewed and told the authorities that he had been fulfilling his duties on the bus which left Gainsborough for Sheffield at six o'clock on the evening of Wednesday, 6 January. It left Retford at 6.45, and Worksop at 7.17, being due at the terminus at Pond Street, Sheffield, at 8.12. He attended an identification parade and saw Nodder. Levick knew him by sight as a passenger who used his bus about once a fortnight, but he had not been on the vehicle throughout this journey. There were several children, including one little girl with fair hair, but she was accompanied by a lady who paid for her ticket, and the other children were likewise in the charge of older persons. There was no man and child together, nor did any little girl travel by herself that night. In his evidence at

Nodder's second trial Levick qualified this statement by admitting that a little girl, aged about twelve, had boarded the bus alone, travelling a short distance, from Osberton to Manton, but he knew her and knew where she was going. The bus conductor's observations were corroborated by other passengers, including a Mrs Wharan. She noticed the fair-haired child and heard her address the lady she was with as 'Mummy'. Mrs Wharan saw no man accompanied by a little girl, nor did she see Nodder. Her daughter Emily, who had been with her, gave similar evidence.

The police realized that they were up against a complete deadlock. This only made them the more eager to solve the mystery. If the child were alive, what had become of her? If she were dead, how and where had her body been concealed? The surrounding country contained unlimited spots in its wildness and desolation where a small corpse could be buried and lie undetected. As well as the local rivers there were gulleys and dykes and the intricacies of Sherwood Forest, to say nothing of lakes and wells. Six of the latter were found within a mile of Peacehaven. On the assumption that Mona Tinsley was dead, boxes and parcels at railway-stations were officially searched, and countless statements were taken from people all over the British Isles who were convinced that they had seen the missing child. All police forces gave ungrudged help and spent an enormous amount of time and care in inquiring into these individual statements. Nothing transpired, and Nodder, the only living soul who knew the truth, remained between prison walls, saying nothing.

Nodder's movements between 5 and 9 p.m. on the 6 January were a mystery. Most of the early part of the day he was seen by neighbours working in his garden. Shortly after twelve o'clock he went to Clarborough and did some small shopping there. He also paid a call at the local inn and returned to his house, having been absent from it about an hour. Mrs Simpson, it appeared, was the last person who actually saw him between 3 p.m. and 3.30. Where was he, and what was he doing, from six o'clock, when the house stood unlighted and presumably empty, and nine, when he was drinking at the Sherwood Foresters' Arms?

If he had murdered the child and disposed of her body by means of burial in the earth, the authorities were certain that his person would have borne traces of the grisly task, yet neither boots nor clothes carried mud or soil when the man was arrested. Neighbouring ditches and hedgerows and adjoining churchyards were carefully examined, but only the bodies of a dog and a sheep were found. A search-party, consisting of between eight and nine hundred persons from Retford, was assembled, and spent a day in exploring a wide area, including coppices and woods. Gravel pits were dug up by the police, and tons of gravel moved. A particular object of suspicion was the adjacent Chesterfield Canal, as it ran within fifty yards of Nodder's house. For weeks this was dragged and a five-mile stretch drained and examined. The water in a culvert running beneath the canal was pumped out after damming, and examination made, without result. Even the appalling weather did not deter the searchers, although it was a time of heavy rains which soon caused extensive flooding. The repeated dragging of the Idle, transformed from a placid stream to a raging river half a mile in width, presented enormous difficulties, grimly faced and overcome. Further exploration of empty properties in the district was made, and cesspools were opened and emptied. Water-bailiffs, gamekeepers, and farmers, as well as agricultural workers were invited to cooperate, but the grim secret remained unsolved.

It is difficult, reviewing the salient events after such a length of time, to realize the enormous excitement and interest aroused not only locally, but all over the British Isles, by the disappearance of an unknown child, a little girl of ten, a member of an obscure working-class family, and the unremitting efforts made to ascertain her fate. The enlisted search-parties and the authorities worked ceaselessly and tirelessly. It was early in the year and truly terrible weather conditions prevailed. The police waded or stood for hours in water and investigated pits, quarries, or any likely spots where a small body might lie hidden. Unsought and unofficial aid was proffered by spiritualists, water-diviners, and mediums. A clairvoyant insisted that Mona Tinsley was dead and had appeared to her. The child declared that she had been strangled, her body placed in a sack, and then conveyed on wheels to the water and thrown in. Another medium told Mr Tinsley that Mona would be found in the River Idle. The medium had tasted mud in her mouth. A third woman informed the Newark police that Mona's body would be recovered in water at a place thirty miles in a north-westerly direction from Newark, 'close to an open meadow or pasture land, with tall trees lining the bank'. In the light of what eventually transpired as to the child's fate these prophecies, made some five months before the truth came to light, are certainly curious.

While the search for Mona Tinsley was being relentlessly pursued, Nodder appeared several times before the magistrates. He applied early for legal aid, on the grounds that he had no means or occupation. After being finally remanded until Tuesday, 16 February, on this date the Bench, without retiring, committed him for trial at the Birmingham Assizes. Nodder renewed his application, which was granted. He pleaded 'Not guilty' and reserved his defence.

*

On 9 March 1937, the trial of Nodder opened at the Warwick Winter Assizes, held at the Victoria Courts, Birmingham. Mr Justice Swift was the presiding judge. Mr Norman Birkett, K.C., and Mr R. E. A. Elwes led for the Crown. The defence was in the hands of Mr Maurice Healy, K.C., and Mr N. F. M. Robinson. The hearing occupied two days, the first being entirely taken up by a lengthy argument between the judge and the senior defending counsel as to the wording of the indictment against the prisoner. The proceedings were chiefly remarkable for the attitude adopted by Mr Justice Swift of universal disapprobation and sarcastic complaint. More than once he declared that he could not hear what was being said by a witness. He insisted that relevant documents had been withheld, and Mr Healy's command of his temper and continued courtesy in the face of incessant fault-finding, correction, and veiled sneers from the Bench were highly commendable. The following passage of arms concluded the first day :

MR JUSTICE SWIFT: What was the subject of that Judgment?

MR MAURICE HEALY: It was on Order XIV proceeding. It was an appealing point. The passages dealing with fraud are of such general application that I venture to state them to your lordship.

MR JUSTICE SWIFT: Such general application to bring an Order XIV case into the Criminal Court at Birmingham Assizes.

MR MAURICE HEALY: My lord, fraud is fraud even in Birmingham.

MR JUSTICE SWIFT: And indeed sometimes I have heard your learned Recorder say it is a good deal more than fraud when it occurs in Birmingham. Now, Mr Healy, how often have you seen an Indictment alleging fraud?

MR MAURICE HEALY: I have seen a certain number, shall I say?

MR JUSTICE SWIFT: Let me see: I, for forty-five years, you for thirty. For thirty years we have been reading Indictments exactly like this. Did anybody think of such an ingenious proposition as what you propose to me?

MR MAURICE HEALY: As your lordship puts that construction upon it, any credit is due to Mr Robinson, but I strongly associate myself with it and I do bear that suggestion in mind, but there is the recent Pepper case tried at the Old Bailey and there most elaborate Particulars were ordered and given.

MR JUSTICE SWIFT: You must forgive me, I am not sufficiently up-to-date. I am not as young as Mr Robinson is. I do not know what happened in the Pepper case at the Old Bailey.

MR MAURICE HEALY: I can only speak *ex relatione*. I understand three prisoners were charged with conspiracy and the conspiracy involved elaborate offences and most elaborate Particulars were ordered and given before the case came to trial.

MR JUSTICE SWIFT: Who ordered them? Ask Mr Robinson who gave them.

MR MAURICE HEALY: They were given by the Prosecution.

MR JUSTICE SWIFT: Does not Mr Robinson know who ordered them? This was so elaborate that something ought to be known about it.

MR MAURICE HEALY: It is not reported, so far as I know. There is no report of it.

MR JUSTICE SWIFT: Ask Mr Robinson who tried the Pepper case.

MR MAURICE HEALY: I am unfortunately not able to offer the information your lordship is seeking with any confidence.

MR JUSTICE SWIFT: You are missing the pepper.

MR MAURICE HEALY: I am not missing the pepper, but I am not able to tell your lordship who was the judge in the case either. I am told it was Mr Justice Humphreys.

MR JUSTICE SWIFT: It does not matter. Mr Robinson has followed the time-honoured tradition of the Bar in stating a case which he knows neither the origin of nor the substance of nor the reference to. But he need not worry, we have all done it.

MR MAURICE HEALY: I do want to do justice to Mr Robinson.

MR JUSTICE SWIFT: You are quite just. He is following the true tradition.

MR MAURICE HEALY: It was I who cited it, and if I was wrong in citing it without full instructions, I must take the blame for it.

MR JUSTICE SWIFT: You know you are going to get nothing out of the application. Why pursue it any further?

MR MAURICE HEALY: If your lordship considers that my client is not embarrassed—

MR JUSTICE SWIFT: I am sure your client is very much embarrassed; to be sitting in the dock and to be charged with fraud is most embarrassing. Your client is embarrassed, but that is no reason why I should make an Order, which I have never heard of in my life – never, and you cannot find one in the books. You may cudgel out of Mr Robinson's brains, but you cannot find in the books the slightest precedent for what you are asking me to do now, and I am not going to do it. There is an end of it, and to Mr Elwes I say you had better put your Indictment in order or you may be in trouble. Is there anything else?

On the second day of the trial Mr Norman Birkett opened the case for the Crown and called as witnesses Mr and Mrs Tinsley, Miss Hawley, Mrs Hird, William Plackett, Charles

Edward Reville, Betts, Whitlam, Cordell, Mrs Simpson, Miss Jarman, Chief Constable Barnes, Police-Constable Coe, Detective-Sergeant Francis, Mrs Grimes, Philip Levick, and Mrs and Miss Wharan. During the evidence of Mrs Grimes a further clash occurred between the judge and defending counsel:

MR MAURICE HEALY: I do not want to muddle up the dates, my lord, but at the same time –

MR JUSTICE SWIFT: You never want to muddle up anything.

MR MAURICE HEALY: I hope, my lord, I never succeed in muddling up anything.

MR JUSTICE SWIFT: Oh, no, you guide and direct me, you never muddle me.

MR MAURICE HEALY: I know that.

MR JUSTICE SWIFT: And you never will, as long as I am here.

MR MAURICE HEALY: Nor shall I ever try, my lord.

MR JUSTICE SWIFT: No, you will not.

The bastardy warrant was produced for the judge's inspection, but its exact nature and contents were not revealed in court. After a further complicated and seemingly interminable argument between Mr Justice Swift and Mr Healy regarding the indictment, the latter announced that he called no evidence for the defence. In his closing speech for Nodder, Mr Healy did not attempt to explain away Mona Tinsley's disappearance, but strove to prove that Nodder had no sinister intention in his mind when he took the child to Peacehaven, and the act had neither force nor fraud behind it. He spoke long and eloquently on his client's behalf, but, as the judge pointed out grimly, why did Nodder, the only person who could really know what had happened to Mona Tinsley, refuse to come forward and in the witness-box say where she was? His summing-up was deadly. The jury took only sixteen minutes to arrive at their verdict. They found the prisoner guilty upon all counts of the indictment. Mr Justice Swift sentenced him to seven years' penal servitude, seven years on the felonies and two years on the misdemeanours, each to run concurrently. The judge's last biting words must have struck doom to the soul of the man in the dock.

> Frederick Nodder, you have been most properly, in my opinion, convicted by the jury of a dreadful crime. What you did with that little girl, what became of her, only you know. It may be that time will reveal the dreadful secret which you carry in your breast. I cannot tell, but I am determined that, as far as I have part or lot in that dreadful tragedy of the 5th January and the 6th January, I will keep you in custody.

Nodder promptly appealed against his conviction and sentence on the grounds of misdirection to the jury by the presiding judge. The hearing opened before the Lord Chief Justice, Mr Justice Humphreys, and Mr Justice Singleton, on 14 April and occupied one day. Nodder maintained by the mouth of his counsel, Mr Healy, that his absence from the witness-box had been adversely commented on by Mr Justice Swift, and the enormous publicity given to the case before the trial opened prejudiced him hopelessly in the eyes of the public. Mr Norman Birkett speedily tore these arguments to shreds, and in giving judgment the Lord Chief Justice voiced it as his and his colleagues' opinion that the summing-up had been eminently fair. The appeal was dismissed and Nodder vanished to serve his sentence. Meanwhile, the search for Mona Tinsley was still being pursued.

*

On the afternoon of Sunday, 6 June 1937, a fine summer day, exactly five months after Mona Tinsley's disappearance, Mr Walter Victor Marshall, who lived at Mellwood, Station Road, Bawtry, and was manager of the local gas-works, took a boating-party, consisting of his wife, his sons, and some friends, for a sail down the River Idle. They embarked at a place on the river known as 'Pilot', at about three o'clock. While going downstream, Mr Marshall noticed an object in the water half to three-quarters of a mile below Bawtry, roughly five yards from the bank on the Nottinghamshire side of the river. This object, when the boat was brought closer, proved to be the body of a child. The legs were floating, or seeking to float, and the head was entirely submerged. The trunk of the body was on the surface of the water, the legs hanging down, and the head appeared to be pulled down well behind the body. The legs were down-stream and the head upstream. Mr Marshall at once sent his son to the police-station at Austerfield, a quarter of a mile east of Bawtry, and P.C. Sheridan, accompanied by other officers, arrived without delay at the spot where the body had been seen. It was lying on its back in the river in about two or three feet of water. The constable was unable to see the head owing to its being submerged. With the assistance of his companions and the aid of Mr Marshall who, obeying police directions, used an oar to dislodge it, he removed the body. The head required to be lifted out of the mud at the bottom of the river. The remains were laid on the bank and after the arrival of Superintendent Burkitt, the Notts County Superintendent of Police, taken under his super-vision to an outhouse at the Ship Inn, Newington. Mr Tins-ley was communicated with and upon seeing the body im-mediately identified it as that of his missing child Mona. The body was clad in the jumper-suit and under-garments which she had been wearing the afternoon she disappeared. The day following the finding of the body, Mr Marshall helped the police to search the river at the spot where the dead child had been lying. He recovered a brown tweed coat from the mud. Police-Constable Slate also came across a Wellington boot in a hole under the water.

On 7 June, Dr James Mathewson Webster, a Registered Medical Practitioner and Director of the West Midland Regional Laboratory, saw the body taken from the Idle on 6 June. The feet had no shoes and stockings and the head no covering; otherwise the body was fully clothed. Before he removed the clothing he noticed on the neck an even mark, darker in colour than the surrounding skin, which ran cir-cularly round the neck. When undressed, the body was found to be in a state of adipocere formation, due to long submersion in the water. It was well nourished, but mud adhered to many portions, on the front, in the eye cavities, between the lips, 'a large deposit', and between the fingers, which were unclenched. The body was removed to the mortuary at Retford, where a post-mortem was conducted by Dr Webster. He came to the conclusion that the mark on the neck had been caused by a ligature, such as string, cord, bootlace, or tape, being tied round it. He found no evidences in the body of natural disease but, based on the condition of the heart and certain teeth indentations which he noticed on the tongue, he considered that Mona Tinsley had not died from drowning, but by strangulation. The act was committed before the child was put into the water. Dr Webster was unable to say precisely how long ago she had been killed.

The inquest on the body of Mona Tinsley was opened at Retford on Tuesday, 8 June. Mr Elliot Warburton, the Retford and District Coroner, sat with a jury of eleven men. The first witness was Superintendent Burkitt, who gave evidence of having gone on Sunday, 6 June, to the Nottinghamshire bank of the River Idle at Scatworth, and seeing the body which had been taken out of the water. He described it as much decomposed. The witness added that he had been present at the post-mortem examination conducted by Dr Webster and assisted by Dr H. S. Holden of Nottingham. At the conclusion of the post-mortem certain organs of the body were removed by Dr Webster for microscopic examination. The Superintendent then produced several articles of clothing identified at Retford Police Station the day before by Mrs Tinsley as the garments worn by her daughter when she last saw her on 5 January. Mr Tinsley, the next witness, stated that he had recognized the child by her clothing, the features, and the hair. After the jury had indicated that they were satisfied as to the identity of the body the coroner adjourned the inquest formally until 20 July. He said that in the meantime proceedings might be taken in another court, in which case the jury would not be troubled again.

Mona Tinsley's body was removed the previous day from

Retford Mortuary to Newark. It remained in the mortuary there while arrangements for the funeral on the forthcoming Thursday were made. She was buried at Newark, following a service at the Methodist Church where she had attended Sunday school. On 29 July, at the police station at Retford, Nodder was charged by Superintendent Burkitt with 'feloniously, wilfully, and of malice aforethought murdering and killing Mona Lilian Tinsley in the County of Nottingham on the 6th of January this year'. Nodder, who had been cautioned before the charge was made, replied that he understood.

Nodder's second trial, on this occasion for the murder of Mona Tinsley, opened on Monday, 22 November 1937, at the Nottingham Assizes. The case, which like its predecessor occupied two days in hearing, was held in the Shire Hall, Nottingham, before Mr Justice Macnaghten. The same counsel as at the previous trial acted for the Crown and the defence. Nodder pleaded 'Not guilty'. Before the jury were sworn, Mr Maurice Healy requested the judge, in view of the tremendous publicity already given to the case, to impress upon the jury that they must exclude from their minds any preconceived opinion based upon information gathered either through the medium of the Press or any private source. This was accordingly done. After a jury had been empanelled and sworn Mr Norman Birkett opened the case for the prosecution, and then called evidence. Amongst the Crown witnesses was Mr Tinsley, who recapitulated the details of Mona's disappearance on 5 January, and identified the various garments taken from the body as what she had been wearing that day. In cross-examination the father agreed to defending counsel's suggestions that Mona was 'very bright', and 'willing to do anything'. Mrs Hird, Mr Barnes, the schoolboy Plackett, the bus conductors and passengers, Nodder's acquaintances Whitlam and Cordell, Mrs Grimes, Mrs Simpson, and Miss Jarman all repeated the testimony they had given at the earlier trial. Mr Marshall described his finding of the body, and Dr Webster his con-

clusions after the post-mortem. ͟ ͟ was ͟ ͟ ͟
witness-box by the famous Sir Berna ͟ ͟ ͟ ͟ ͟
roborated these entirely. The theory of ͟ ͟ ͟ ͟
mark upon the dead child's neck had b ͟ ͟ ͟ ͟
dress catching upon a branch, so that sh ͟ ͟ ͟
from it for some minutes before falling into ͟ ͟ ͟ ͟
Bernard refuted utterly.

Superintendent Burkitt was closely examined ͟ ͟ cross-
examined as to the locality where the body was found. On
5 and 6 January the River Idle had been very swollen. Water
came to the top of the bank, but did not overflow it. The
nearest point of the Idle to Peacehaven, Nodder's ill-named
house, was Bolham Shuttle, 1·9 miles distant. A metalled
road ran all the way. This road was dry on the Wednesday
night owing to the high wind. The Ryton flowed through
Worksop and joined the Idle near Bawtry at Scrooby. A
person leaving Nodder's house would go along Smeath Lane,
a little of Tiln Lane, and then Bolham Lane. In Smeath
Lane there was a house, Lowfield, standing back from the
road, and Bolham Cottage Farm in the same position, but
the witness described the way from Peacehaven to Bolham
Shuttle as 'a deserted road'. It was dark and there were no
lamps. A small public house, the Gate Inn, was not immediately on the road, and had hardly any customers until nine
o'clock at night. Nodder had not been to the Criterion, but
was proved to have visited the Sherwood Foresters' Arms
arriving at 9 p.m. and leaving an hour later. The distance to
this licensed house from Bolham Shuttle was about three-
quarters of a mile. In cross-examination the Superintendent
disagreed with defending counsel's suggestions that anybody
using that road would have had mud or matter from the
sewage works on his boots.

On the second day of the trial, the accused, the sole witness for the defence, gave evidence. Examined by Mr Healy,
Nodder described himself as a motor-engineer. He told of his
brief stay at the Tinsley's house in 1935, and his becoming
acquainted with the children, including Mona. He was 'a bit

money', and left through being unable to pay his
but maintained that there was no bad feeling on this
account or any other between himself and Mr and Mrs
Tinsley. In June of 1936 he went to live at Peacehaven, and
here Mrs Grimes – Mrs Tinsley's sister – continued the visits
she had begun to make him earlier in the year at his previous
address. He was proposing to buy a motor-lorry, and Mrs
Grimes was willing to help him to pay the instalments on the
purchase. On 2 January, the Saturday before the 5th, he
saw Mrs Grimes, who promised to bring him some money on
the following Wednesday (the 6th). On the Tuesday (the
5th) Mrs Grimes rang him up at Mrs Simpson's and Nodder
told her that he was prepared to buy the lorry, and inquired
if, as co-partner, she wanted one of any particular colour.
She left the point to him, repeated that she would bring the
money the next day, and rang off. The same morning,
Nodder went from Retford to Carlton in quest of a Mr Teal,
the owner of certain gravel-pits, who might give him some
work. Mr Teal had an office in Newark, and on finding that
he had been by accident conveyed a mile in the bus beyond
his destination, Carlton, Nodder decided to go on to Newark
and arrived there about midday. After lunching at a café
next door to Newark G.P.O. he went down to the wharf in
search of Mr Teal. He was unable to get in touch with him,
but noted his address and telephone number. Afterwards he
visited the public library. He left just before four o'clock,
and until his bus went – 'I was under the impression that
it was quarter to four to quarter to five' – took a stroll
round the town. Suddenly a child accosted him, saying
'Hullo, Uncle Fred!' He recognized Mona Tinsley and asked
how she was getting on. Mona inquired for her aunt Mrs
Grimes and expressed a wish to see her small cousin Peter,
Mrs Grimes's baby. Nodder 'allowed himself to be persuaded
to take her', though he warned the child that Mrs Grimes
was not at Newark and she could not see her aunt until the
next day. They travelled by bus to Retford, and he bought
some food at a shop, Walker's, in Cannon Square. He did

not remember seeing Whitlam, nor did he hear Whitlam
calling out to him. Mona and he reached Peacehaven between seven and seven-thirty. They had supper and went to
bed about nine o'clock. He slept downstairs and Mona had
the double bed upstairs. Next morning she came to breakfast
and washed up for him afterwards. About 8 a.m. the post
brought a letter from Mrs Grimes. Nodder burned it, as he
did all her letters. Now realizing that he had acted very
foolishly in bringing the child away with him he decided to
take or send her to her aunt in Sheffield. Asked why he
settled on this course instead of returning Mona to her
parents, Nodder explained that he wanted Mrs Grimes to
act as a mediator. It was a cold, windy day, though not
actually raining, and Mona was playing about the house,
'reading books and writing', while he worked in his garden.
They had dinner in the middle of the day, 'some pork pie,
and things like that'. He was reluctant to go into Sheffield
because of a warrant for his committal in respect of non-
payment of a sum of eighteen pounds, and 'going on for six
o'clock' decided to take Mona part of the way himself and
then entrust her to the care of a Mr Brookes at Worksop for
the rest of the journey. He did not know Mr Brookes's
private address, but trusted to finding him at his place of
business. Mona and he left Peacehaven between six and
seven, and at Retford boarded a bus for Sheffield. He was
not very familiar with the service. On the bus Nodder
'changed his mind' about seeking Mr Brookes and decided
to let Mona complete the journey to Sheffield and her aunt's
house by herself. He gave her both written and verbal directions as to how to reach her destination and provided her
with two shillings to cover her bus and tram fares. In addition he gave her an explanatory letter for Mrs Grimes. At
Worksop he alighted, intending to take a bus back to Retford. Mona remained on the Sheffield-bound one. As far as
he knew it went on, but he did not stay to see it re-start. He
never saw Mona again. He reached Retford about half past
eight and had a drink at the Criterion. Then he went on to

the Sherwood Foresters' Arms, where he remained until closing time, ten o'clock. He walked home and had the encounter
with Mr Barnes. When they entered the house, Mr Barnes
'pushed the commitment order in front of my face', and said
he supposed that Nodder had not the money for it. Nodder
replied that he had not, and then the Chief Constable
'started talking about Mona'. He could not hear what was
said owing to being 'very upset'. Nodder acknowledged that
he denied having seen Mona or knowing anything of her
whereabouts. Later, he asked for Mrs Grimes to be brought
over from Sheffield, and the statement he made in her
presence was true. He denied that he had ever done anything to Mona Tinsley which could have caused her harm
'because I thought too much about her'.

In cross-examination by Mr Birkett, Nodder stuck to his
story that he had decided his best course was to send Mona
to her aunt at Sheffield instead of taking her back to her
parents. He was upset by the committal order's production
and consequently lied when he denied all knowledge of her.
He 'did not know' why he had not explained frankly what
had occurred. He 'never gave it a thought' that Mrs Tinsley
would be upset and distressed if Mona did not return when
he had agreed to take her to see her aunt. There would not
have been time, he averred, to walk home with the child and
ask her mother's leave. Not until he got back to Peacehaven
did he realize that Mrs Tinsley might be very anxious about
Mona. He denied that Mrs Hird had seen him in Guildhall
Street about four o'clock, and said he did not know that
Mona attended the Wesleyan School. He had made no
preparations at his home for Mona. It did not occur to him
to consult Mrs Simpson, his next-door neighbour, who had
a little girl of her own, in his dilemma, nor did it occur to
him to telephone a wire to Mona's parents from Mrs Simpson's. After he received Mrs Grimes's letter next morning,
saying that she was not coming over, he decided to send
Mona to Sheffield instead of taking her home. He did not
want to go to Sheffield in the daylight because of the com-

mittal order against him. He 'could not say' why he did not take her as far as Worksop in the daytime, but waited until darkness.

Mr Healy's re-examination was very brief and dealt mainly with the alleged 'shock' of seeing the committal order, and the whereabouts of Mr Brookes. In his defence of Nodder his counsel advanced the theory that Mona Tinsley on her way to Sheffield had been lured from the bus by some stranger and he, not Nodder, committed the crime.

After counsel for either side had addressed the jury, Mr Justice Macnaghten began his summing-up. His cold logic tore to fragments the frail fabric erected by the defence, and exposed mercilessly the hollowness of the prisoner's story and statements. After he had dismissed the jury to consider their verdict they were recalled about half an hour later to hear further evidence by Mr Marshall. The witness stated that in the middle of May, some weeks before his discovery of Mona Tinsley's body in the Idle, he was boating on the Ryton and ran aground on a sandbank just prior to getting to Scrooby Mill. As he was pushing-off, he and his sons, who were with him, observed in the water a sack which emitted a disagreeable odour. It was approximately the size which would hold a hundredweight of potatoes. In reply to the question, 'Would it be big enough to contain the body of a child?' witness replied, 'I should imagine so.' The boating-party pushed it away into the silt and did not see it again. This sack looked like a potato sack and the offensive smell was noticeable to all of them. The defence's contention in calling this further evidence was that the sack might have held the body of Mona Tinsley, and that it had been put into the River Ryton and not into the Idle. The Ryton flows through Worksop, joining the Idle near Bawtry at Scrooby. Nodder had averred that he parted from Mona Tinsley at Worksop. The judge considered 'that it was not a matter which was of primary importance to the case'. He sent the jury back to continued their deliberations. They retired again at 4.24 and returned with their verdict of 'Guilty' at 5.3.

Nodder, asked whether he had anything to say, replied, 'I shall go out of this court with a clear conscience, sir.' Mr Justice Macnaghten sentenced him to death very briefly. His few words before passing sentence were memorable. 'Frederick Nodder, the jury by their verdict have found that you murdered Mona Lilian Tinsley. Justice has slowly but surely overtaken you, and it only remains for me to pronounce the sentence which the law and justice require.' Time – a bare five months – had indeed revealed the dreadful secret which Nodder carried in his breast.

His appeal against his conviction and sentence was heard on 13 December, before the Lord Chief Justice (Lord Hewart of Bury), Mr Justice Branson, and Mr Justice Porter. The summing-up of Mr Justice Macnaghten was described as 'most admirable and careful', and the plea of misdirection to the jury was completely rejected. The appeal was dismissed without hesitation. On 30 December, Nodder was executed at Lincoln Prison, having survived by two months Mr Justice Swift, who sentenced him at his first trial. As he went to his doom did the stern words of the presiding judge at his second one ring in his ears : 'Justice has slowly but surely overtaken you'? Did he perchance think of other words, uttered two thousand years ago : 'It is impossible but that offences will come : but woe unto him, through whom they come! It were better for him that a millstone were hanged about his neck, and he cast into the sea, than that he should offend one of these little ones'?

What really chanced that dark, windy January night in the sordid, semi-detached, commonplace house? No one will ever know for certain. When found, the child's body was too decomposed for medical knowledge to establish whether before her death she had been criminally assaulted, but taking into account Nodder's character, his strong sexual tendencies particularly, the most likely supposition is that this occurred, Mona Tinsley afterwards being strangled by her assailant to ensure her silence. She was last seen alive and well at twelve o'clock. At seven the same night the police arrived. An hour earlier there was no light in the house. One pictures this evil man lurking there, the body of his victim hidden in a sack, and directly darkness fell stealing forth with his dreadful burden. Along the hard, lampless, unfrequented road the murderer hurries, panting and stumbling, casting fearful glances towards isolated farm, unlit cottage, or silent inn. The wind roars and buffets him as he stands on the verge of that swollen river and heaves into it something which a few hours earlier had been alive and happy. What should he do now that his ghastly secret seems safe? He craves for lights, companionship, liquor. In the Sherwood Foresters Arms he finds all these and lingers until the last permissible second. Then back to the squalid little house where, though he does not know it, Nemesis is waiting. Nodder has not time to concoct the story he told later and impulsively denies all knowledge of the child he had so lately robbed of chastity and life.

The place where the cruel deed was really committed remains a mystery. Did Nodder strangle the child in the house? A theory held by the police was that he possessed himself of some vehicle, conveyed his little victim in it to a spot near the Idle, and there murdered her and threw the body into the river. Alternatively, he killed her at Peacehaven between midday and 6 p.m. and took her, dead, to the water, probably in a sack. She would not be a heavy burden for a man of Nodder's build and strength.

Was Nodder's fearful crime a deliberately premeditated one? Did he go to Newark that day with black purpose – rape, if not murder – in his heart? He denied that he knew of Mona Tinsley's attending the Wesleyan School, but why, as observed by Mrs Hird, was he loitering in Guildhall Street, watching the school door out of which the children must presently emerge? What bait did he employ to induce the child to accompany him? It was growing dark and she would naturally wish to hurry home to her mother and her tea. None of the witnesses who saw her on the bus or running behind Nodder after alighting from the vehicle noticed any signs of reluctance or fear about her. No doubt she enjoyed the holiday stolen from school, and Nodder may have invented some plausible story which soothed any disquiet she might have harboured on her parents' account. Possibly Nodder was suffering from disappointment at some hitch in his sordid plans, and Mona Tinsley served to whet his frustrated appetite. The man was described as a monster by the prosecuting counsel's clerk who observed him closely during his trial for murder, though no suggestion that Nodder was otherwise than completely sane was ever put forward. A study of his mind and mentality brings out that he was in no way unbalanced, but horribly abnormal in a particular respect, and this brought Mona Tinsley to her doom.

Peter Barnes and Others

(The I.R.A. Coventry Explosion of 1939)

BY

LETITIA FAIRFIELD

On the afternoon of 25 August 1939, a bomb exploded in the main street of the pleasant city of Coventry, killing five people and injuring about sixty others, besides doing much damage to property. The victims were chance passers-by, all quite unknown to the perpetrators of the explosion. It was the most impersonal and anonymous of crimes, of interest because of the unusual problem of detection which it presented, and also because of the historical background which furnished its only motive.

In the 800-year-long struggle for Irish independence, very seldom have active hostilities taken place on the soil of Britain. The first that can be traced was in connexion with the Fenian Rising of 1867, and even then it was more by accident than design that any part of the military operations took place in England itself. After the collapse of the Rising, the leader of the Irish Republican Brotherhood, a man named Kelly, escaped to England and was arrested by the police in Manchester in company with an Irish-American officer, one Deasy. Command of the scattered rebels was then in the hands of a certain Colonel Ricard O'Sullivan Burke, a picturesque soldier of fortune who had fought for the North in the American Civil War. The presence of so many ex-Civil War officers among the Fenians is explained by the fact that the Fenian Brotherhood had recruited thousands of men on both sides in that campaign. Many of them came to Ireland to assist in the Rising. Burke had recently been successfully buying arms for the Fenians in Birmingham. To him occurred the daring notion of rescuing the two prisoners from the prison van while they were being taken from the Manchester Court. With the help of some thirty members of his organization armed with revolvers, hatchets, and stones, he achieved his purpose. Kelly and Deasy escaped, but the police officer in charge of the van, Sergeant Brett, had been killed when the door was blown open. Of the men arrested on the spot, five were charged with murder and sentenced to death. One of the convicted prisoners, a marine named Maguire, was pardoned as it was found that he had nothing to do with the riot; another man, Edward Meagher Condon (an American subject), was reprieved; and three men, William Philip Allen, Michael O'Brien (also an ex-Civil-War Officer), and Michael Larkin, were hanged.

The justice of these executions has always been passionately contested in Ireland on the ground that although all three men were members of the attacking party, the death of Sergeant Brett was not intended and the fatal shot was actually fired by a man not in custody. By British law both these points were irrelevant. It is admitted that 'Colonel Burke had given strict orders that no life was to be taken, unless it was imperative for the success of the rescue but in that case there was to be no hesitation' (Desmond Ryan, *The Phoenix Flame*). As Mr Justice Blackburn put it in addressing the jury, 'if they were satisfied from the evidence that the prisoners had gone with a design to liberate Kelly and Deasy with dangerous violence, and death ensued therefrom, they would be right in returning a verdict of murder'. These fundamentally different conceptions of the law of murder, the cause of so much discord in the past century, emerged again in the trial of Barnes and Richards and will be discussed in that connexion.

The unhappy aftermath of the Fenian Rising was not concluded yet. Shortly after the Manchester executions, Colonel Burke and a man named Casey were arrested, charged with buying arms, and lodged in the Clerkenwell House of Detention (in the north of London) to await trial.

In an effort to repeat the triumph of the Manchester rescue a certain Jeremiah O'Sullivan, chief or 'centre' of the local Fenians, and a Captain Murphy pushed a barrel containing 548 lb. of gunpowder up against the wall of the prison and set light to it, with the appalling results that might have been expected. Widespread destruction of property followed, about one hundred people were injured, and a number, variously estimated at between five and twelve, were killed. Fortunately for themselves, Burke and Casey were not in the exercise ground as had been intended; they had been confined to their cells, as the Governor had been warned that there would be an attempt at rescue.

The Clerkenwell explosion embittered British feeling against the Irish Nationalists nearly as much as the Manchester executions had embittered Irish feeling. Much mystery still surrounds the episode, for Jeremiah O'Sullivan later claimed that Burke himself had directed the attempted rescue from his cell, and no experienced military engineer would give such suicidal orders. Either there was a complete misunderstanding of instructions, or Burke was already showing signs of the mental derangement which overtook him after his committal to prison on a fifteen-year sentence. It was a culminating misfortune that the guilt of the man (Michael Barrett) convicted and hanged for complicity in the explosion remains in the gravest doubt; one would have to go far to find a trial with such an atmosphere of perjury.

There followed a fifteen-year interval without disturbance of the domestic peace of Britain, and the next threats were to come not from Ireland itself but from the United States. The part played by the United States in the movements of Irish independence was an inevitable result of the great flow of immigrants it received all through the nineteenth century, many of them taking bitter memories into exile. The Wild Geese who, in the eighteenth century, had scattered over Europe now flew westward in flocks that darkened the sky. They and their children had eagerly supported the Fenians as offering an immediate hope for the liberation of their

country, but after the failures of the invasions of Canada in
1866 and 1870 and of the 1867 rising in Ireland the Brotherhood had inevitably to face reorganization. Ultimately the
great bulk of the members united to form the Clan-na-Gael,
a militant separatist association very similar in structure and
objects to the original Fenian Brotherhood. Some small
'splinter' organizations still retained an independent existence, but all were still covered by the popular name 'Fenian'.
The affiliated organization in Ireland was known as the Irish
Republican Brotherhood.

During the seventies, under the leadership of John Devoy
and other exiles from British gaols, the Clan was fully occupied in building up a huge organization with branches
('Camps') which extended from ocean to ocean. It obtained
an enormous influence in American politics, local and
national, it infiltrated the constitutional Irish associations in
the U.S.A., and it gave valiant support to the movements
active in Ireland. But this was not enough to satisfy the eager
aspirations of the American Irish; a new generation was
clamouring for vigorous action against England. Enormous
funds had been collected for this very purpose – why were
they not being used? The older Fenians who had settled in
Paris and New York were, however, firmly opposed to another head-on collision with the growing might of the British
Empire. They urged delay until England was entangled in a
continental war; too well did they know just how disastrous
militant action could be for the weaker party in the combat.

The form that the enterprise ultimately took was determined, as are so many events in history, by an apparently
remote advance in scientific knowledge. In the middle of the
nineteenth century developments in the manufacture of high
explosives had made possible the use of portable bombs
which could be thrown or deposited in public places with
deadly effect. We are now so accustomed to think of the
bomb in terms of the atomic bomb that one forgets that
bombs appeared to the nineteenth-century revolutionary as
the poor man's friend. They were a means whereby the

mighty could be put down from their seats, a sign that God is
not always on the side of the big battalions. The gospel of
social and political redemption by dynamite brought to New
York by exiles from Russia and Germany seemed to the
hesitating stalwarts of the Clan-na-Gael the answer to their
problem. But they met with much opposition, even from
those Irish-Americans conspicuous for a passionate hostility
to British rule and for a belief in physical force. Most of the
older men repudiated a policy of terrorism with disgust. Old
John O'Leary described O'Donovan Rossa's support of
dynamite as 'let us hope mostly mere talk, but very wicked
talk indeed'.

A complete reorganization of the Clan was therefore
necessary before a bombing policy could be carried out, and
in 1881 the opportunity came. At the Chicago Clan Con-
vention that year the old guard was ousted and the control of the huge organization and its vast funds passed into
the hands of a small clique led by an ill-omened figure,
a very astute and ruthless Canadian-born lawyer, Alexander
Sullivan. Thereafter the preparations for a terrorist campaign in England went rapidly ahead.

It did not fall to the Clan-na-Gael to strike the first blow.
That flamboyant personality, O'Donovan Rossa, who had
quarrelled with the Clan and who was now a leader of a
vaguely constituted group containing the remnants of the
original Fenian Brotherhood, is suspected of responsibility
for the first campaign, a forgotten but highly significant
episode. It started, of all unlikely places, on Glasgow Green
in June 1882, when two 'fine gentlemen from America'
giving their names as Timothy Featherstone and Henry
Dalton or Johnstone got into touch with a small group of
Irish labourers who belonged to some obscure 'Ribbon
Society'. Their real names were Edmund O'Brien Kennedy
and John Henry O'Connor. It is not yet certain who sent
them. The picture presented at the subsequent trial of these
wretchedly poor, decent, illiterate exiles reminds one vividly
that this whole story must be seen against a background of

centuries of misgovernment, of religious and social oppression, of evictions and unwilling emigration, and above all of a frustrated desire for self-government. Through the agency of these 'Ribbon' men, led by a workman named Terence M'Dermott, the American emissaries managed to buy considerable quantities of chemicals necessary for the manufacture of explosives. Part of these materials were retained in Glasgow, where they were converted into bombs by the workmen in their houses. On 20 January 1883 there occurred the only explosions recorded as taking place on Scottish soil. The sites were the Lilybank Road gas-works, the Possil Bridge aqueduct, and a shed at Buchanan Street Station. Fortunately little damage was done and no lives were lost. The police had no clue whatever to the perpetrators of the incidents.

The bulk of the Glasgow chemicals were consigned to Cork, where Featherstone and a colleague named Deasy busied themselves early in 1883 in the manufacture of crude types of bombs. At this stage they were unlucky enough to encounter a notorious scoundrel, one 'Red Jim' M'Dermott, drunkard, informer, and *agent provocateur*. He seems to have won their confidence by introductions given by indiscreet Fenians in New York, and as a result, Featherstone was arrested in Cork on 29 March with recipes for bomb-making in his pocket; Deasy had been taken the previous day on landing at Liverpool in possession of what counsel at the Scottish trial described as 'a most wicked sort of luggage'; 'Henry Dalton' or O'Connor was arrested in London, where he had probably been responsible for the explosion at *The Times* office. M'Dermott could have known nothing of the Glasgow end of the conspiracy, for their unhappy confederates in that city were not discovered until August, and then only because a £500 reward induced one of their number to turn informer. Ten of them went to penal servitude.

Just as this conspiracy broke down, a small expeditionary force dispatched by the Clan-na-Gael landed at Liverpool on 26 March. The leaders were a keen and capable Dr Gallagher and a technical expert named Alfred Whitehead, who was already at work in Birmingham. Half a dozen assistants trained in bomb-setting accompanied them. The English police, who knew all about their arrival, waited long enough for Whitehead to manufacture a huge quantity of nitro-glycerine, long enough for their supporters in this country to be identified – then on 5 April drew in the net and made a memorable haul. By a great stroke of luck for the authorities the first man arrested (one Norman or Lynch) turned Queen's Evidence and saved them the painful necessity of revealing their more important sources of information. The four chief plotters (Gallagher, Whitehead, Curtin, and Wilson) were sentenced to confinement for life. It is stated that on their release in 1896 Gallagher and Whitehead were found to be insane. One can well believe that the horrors of a convict prison in the eighties were too much for men unused to hardship. 'Thomas Wilson, clerk' was the *nom de guerre* of Thomas J. Clarke, one of the chief leaders of the Easter Week Rising. He was executed in April 1916. His widow was elected the first woman Lord Mayor of Dublin as late as 1939.

As a result of these disasters the American organization changed its plans and thenceforward sent its emissaries not 'in battalions' but as 'single spies'. This method brought a little more success; during 1884 there were some half-dozen explosions in public places (causing, it is true, very little damage), and a few of the dynamitards who operated alone managed to escape back to the United States. But when in December 1884 a much esteemed veteran of the Fenian Rising, one William Mackay Lomasney, blew himself and another man to fragments in an attempt on London Bridge, the campaign was abandoned. No doubt the realization that the outrages were damaging the Liberal Party's long over-due programme of reforms in Ireland, as well as the position of the Irish Parliamentary Party, had much to do with the decision. To mark the Queen's Jubilee in 1887 several factions of the New York extremists combined to attempt another terrorist demonstration under the leadership of a General Millen and J. J. Moroney of the Clan-na-Gael. Once again the plotters were seized before any but negligible damage was done. The ringleaders escaped back to the United States, one man died in London, and two minor figures went to join their comrades in penal servitude. It is some measure of the failure of terrorism that there were at the moment 'twenty-five of the unfortunate instruments in prison, sixteen undergoing life sentences, two sentences of twenty years penal servitude, and seven sentences of seven years each'. Not a single British life had been lost and no damage of any importance had been done. For the next fifty years the advocates of Irish independence attempted no more acts of violence on British soil, with the exception of a terrible but fortunately unique episode, the assassination of Field-Marshal Sir Henry Wilson in 1922 by two Irish ex-servicemen resident in London.

The story of the dynamitards would be incomplete without some account of the remarkable events at the American end of the conspiracy. The unbroken series of disasters had naturally produced the liveliest reaction in the revolutionary organizations. Like later and more welcome American visitors, the dynamitards had learnt that our 'English police are wonderful', but, as they rightly suspected, not as wonderful as all that without considerable help from inside information. At first 'Red Jim' M'Dermott was made the universal scapegoat, but although he had been a considerable nuisance, the facts pointed inexorably to some figure better placed in the organization. Even Alexander Sullivan found himself the object of suspicion, especially after his reputation had been shaken by charges of dubious dealings in the vast funds under control of himself and the other two members of the all-powerful Executive, known as the 'Triangle' (Sullivan, Feeley, and Boland). His enemies, led by Dr Philip Cronin, insisted on an inquiry being held into the management of the Clan-na-Gael, and as an upshot Boland was dismissed for peculation, and Feeley and Sullivan were censured (August 1888).

Not until February 1889 was the mystery of the leakage explained. The Parnell Commission was then meeting in London and there suddenly appeared as a witness against Parnell a Major Henry Le Caron. Thomas Beach was his real name. He was born in Colchester in 1841, had fought for the North in the American Civil War, and was known to some of the astounded onlookers as a 'Senior Guardian' of a Clan-na-Gael Camp, a trusted friend of Alexander Sullivan and other high-ranking leaders. For twenty-five years, so it appeared, Le Caron had been a Secret Service Agent, the channel whereby all the routine orders of the Clan and many of its most confidential plans had reached Sir Robert Anderson of Scotland Yard. He had never been one of the inmost circle of the Clan-na-Gael and neither knew nor purported to know all its secrets, but he had known more than enough to enable the police to defeat the dynamite campaign. Le Caron also revealed the plans of both the Fenian invasions of Canada (1866 and 1870). These totally unexpected revelations came too late to do Sullivan or the Clan much good; the storms of hatred and jealousy had run too high. When a few months later (April 1889) the naked body of Dr Cronin was found in a Chicago reservoir and a coroner's jury returned a verdict of wilful murder against Sullivan, he knew, though he was never brought to trial, that his bright day was over and he was for the dark. Thanks to the loyalty of the Irish population in the United States, the Clan-na-Gael recovered in time from the body blows to its reputation; it found worthier leaders, and became once again a very important factor in the fight for Irish independence. But it never again ventured on direct militant action on British territory.

*

The long and tangled chain of events which led up to the partitioning of Ireland into Eire and Northern Ireland is no part of this narrative, still less are the merits of the dispute. It is necessary, however, to discuss briefly the attitude of the Irish Republican Army, the organization responsible for the bombing campaign. The I.R.A. in 1939 saw themselves not only as a militant resistance movement but as the heirs of the original Irish Republic declared in 1916, and therefore the *de jure* rulers of all Ireland. In practise they represented the irreconcilable residue of Republican separatists who objected not only to the presence of British authority on any part of Irish soil (for in that respect they were at one with every other political party in Eire), but also to the retention of any link between Eire and the Commonwealth. On this latter point they were in disagreement with the Eire Government. True, the Taoiseach (Eamonn de Valera) had, ever since his accession to power in 1932, been engaged in severing painlessly nearly all the ties forged by the Treaties of 1921 and 1925, and in substituting 'for a fetter, a silken thread of diplomatic cooperation – to be used or broken at Ireland's will'.* True, also, that by 1939 the silken thread had become as tenuous as a cobweb, for the revision of the Eire constitution two years earlier had eliminated the very name of the King and reduced him to a functionless 'organ or instrument of association'. But even this compromise appeared so intolerable to the fundamentalists of the I.R.A. that they felt justified in permanent hostility (even in armed hostility) to the Eire Government as well as to the Government which ruled Ulster under the Union Jack. In Northern Ireland also trouble was never far below the surface; in 1935 and 1936 there had been a recrudescence of serious disturbance with armed violence used on both sides. At the time the campaign against England opened in 1939 the I.R.A. had long been proclaimed an illegal organization and there were thirty-four persons in prison in Belfast under Special Powers Acts, 1922–3.

* Miss Dorothy MacCardle, *With Fanfares*. The thread was finally broken in 1948 when Eire became a completely independent Republic.

Two factors combined to divert the attention of the physical force Republican section to England at this juncture. The first was the troubled European situation, which could have only one message to those brought up in the faith, that 'England's danger is Ireland's opportunity'. They remembered 1916 and burned to stage another Easter Week. But history needs to be mixed, as Sir Joshua Reynolds claimed that he mixed his paints, 'with brains, sir', if it is to be a safe guide and not a snare. The I.R.A. failed to see that time had marched on, that Irishmen of the type available for armed revolt in 1916 were now serving their country in the other ways open to them now but not then. If they took up arms again it would be at the bidding of their own responsible government, not at the invitation of an irresponsible group without authority. Moreover, the issues at stake were now less compelling as a call to the shedding of blood, to the risks of life imprisonment – or the gallows. In respect of England the miscalculations of the I.R.A. were even greater. The few previous attempts at terrorism in that country had never had the slightest success; calculated terrorism is by no means the same thing as an individual gesture of rage and despair, or an armed revolt, and evokes a wholly different response. The I.R.A. appeared to have reckoned, however, that England in 1939 was in such a state of jitters in face of the Nazi menace that she would belie her past and yield to any action threatening her war preparations. The fact was that not for many years had the country been more nationally alert, more united in confidence in the rightness of her cause. It was indeed the most unlikely moment in history when any nation so circumstanced would have agreed to expel loyal citizens anxious to remain under its flag, to surrender valuable territory held unbrokenly for 800 years, and to create grave internal disorder; and that is how the British saw the situation. After these miscalculations it may be considered only a minor lapse from realism that the I.R.A. should have expected that Germany would give their campaign effective support, even without any *quid pro quo* in the way of promised help in case of war. Minds that could picture Eamonn de Valera as the feeble tool of the British Government naturally had no difficulty in visualizing Hitler as the disinterested friend of small nationalities.

The personalities and indeed the very names of the men who made these decisions were then, and are now, almost unknown to the public. Only one name aroused a faint echo outside Ireland, and he was an individual of such vigour and experience that his appointment as Chief of Staff of the I.R.A. in 1938 formed the second of the factors which impelled that organization to militant action. Sean Russell had been on active service, either in the field or in prison, ever since 1916 when as a member of the Irish Volunteers (known from 1921 as the Irish Republican Army) he had taken part in the Easter Week Rising. He was soon appointed Director of Munitions, a post he held with great success through the long struggle with the British Army and the Black and Tans, and later (under the banner of Mr de Valera) against the pro-Treaty party in the tragic civil war of 1922 to 1925. But when Mr de Valera decided to abandon hostilities, to take the oath, and to enter the Dail Eireann, Sean Russell was amongst those of the I.R.A. who stood apart from the former leaders and refused to compromise either in demands or in methods. For him there was only one issue in the world, a completely separate Republic for an undivided Ireland, and only one method of getting it – unceasing attacks on England.

Sean Russell's assets as a leader were not only his unique experience in the supply of munitions for an 'underground', but his gift for inspiring men to astonishing sacrifice in the shape of austere and dangerous living. Unfortunately for his cause, those very virtues of highly specialized experience and single-minded devotion were to prove a handicap in the supreme leadership of a movement : even a revolution cannot be successfully conducted in blinkers. But he did manage to recruit and train several hundred men and women for his hopeless enterprise.

The capture of the 'S Plan' at an early stage of the campaign gave a valuable glimpse of the outlook of these modern terrorists. The document shows some traces of military staff training ('S' probably stands for 'Staff') and may be the work of Russell himself. It is an interesting warning of the vulnerability of a complex industrial civilization to sabotage, provided (and this is where the I.R.A. failed) that there has been sufficient infiltration of the attacking party into the texture of the State. That the section on Propaganda in the S Plan is left blank is significant. The I.R.A. either had no adequate channels for informing the public of the reason for the campaign or did not use them. From beginning to end acts of violence appeared to the British people as meaningless and wanton. The only effect could be to etch the Border more deeply on the map of Ireland.

*

Hostilities were opened formally with a shot fired across the bows of the British Commonwealth. On 12 January 1939, an 'ultimatum' was addressed to the Prime Minister and copies were sent to the Foreign Secretary, the Government of Northern Ireland, the German Führer, the Italian Duce, and sundry other notabilities. The terms of the communication were as follows :

I have the honour to inform you that the Government of the Irish Republic, having as its first duty towards the people the establishment and maintenance of peace and order, herewith demand the withdrawal of all British armed forces stationed in Ireland. These forces are an active incitement to turmoil and civil strife not only in being a symbol of hostile occupation but in their effect and potentialities as an invading army.

It is secondly the duty of the Government to establish relations of friendship between the Irish and all other peoples. We must insist on the withdrawal of British troops from our country and a declaration from your Government renouncing all claims to interfere in our domestic policy.

The letter declared that neither the Government of the

Irish Republic nor the Irish people were actuated by any feelings of hostility towards England.

We shall regret if this fundamental feeling is ignored and we are compelled to intervene actively in the military and commercial life of your country as your Government are now intervening in ours.

. The Government of the Irish Republic believe that a period of four days is sufficient for your Government to signify its intention in the matter of the military evacuation and for the issue of your declaration of abdication in respect of our country. Our Government reserves the right of appropriate action without further notice if on the expiration of the period of grace these conditions remain unfulfilled.

(Signed) STEPHEN HAYES
PEADER O'FLAHERTY
LAURENCE GROGAN
PATRICK FLEMING
GEORGE PLUNKETT
SEAN RUSSELL

It is doubtful if any of the addressees (except in Northern Ireland) were allowed by their amused subordinates to see these documents, which looked much like the kind of practical joke not uncommonly played on public officials. But when four days later, on 16 January, many copies of a Proclamation in similar terms appeared on the walls of Eire and Northern Ireland and a few in Great Britain, and a series of widely distributed bomb explosions broke the early morning calm, it was clear that something serious was afoot. In London three explosions occurred at electricity plants, and in the North and Midlands many gas and electricity mains were damaged. One tragic incident should have warned the conspirators at the outset that their expressed purpose of playing with high explosives without taking life was a dream of impossible fulfilment. A bomb deposited in a street main in Manchester killed a twenty-seven-year-old fish porter named Albert Ross, abroad in the early morning on his lawful occasions, and injured two other persons.

For the next fifteen months the system of sabotage outlined in the S Plan was steadily carried out, mainly in London, the Midlands, and the North. A bewildered public became accustomed to being confronted by machines of destruction in places it had never specifically associated with the Border, such as public lavatories, telephone boxes, railway cloakrooms, pillar-boxes, cinemas, post-offices, and business premises. In a few instances tear-gas bombs were used, and many incendiaries were planted, but the commonest weapon of I.R.A. warfare was the time-bomb, embodying an alarm clock set in a circuit with a halfpenny. Someone had blundered over these supplies, for the clocks were of such miserable quality that they often failed to go off at all; but for this misplaced economy disasters would have been more frequent and serious.

It was remarkable how little disturbance of public life or business routine the whole futile affair caused. No major effort from beginning to end came off as was intended. Several attempts were made at blowing up bridges (notably an attack on Hammersmith Bridge in March 1939), and canals and aqueducts were also threatened, but, as military engineers know, these structures are not so easy to destroy as one might think. One of the worst episodes was staged on 24 June, when four serious explosions occurred in London and some damage to property was done; the bomb planted in Piccadilly Circus deprived a passer-by of an eye. On 26 July came a repetition of the Manchester disaster. An explosion in the left-luggage office at King's Cross station killed a traveller on holiday from Edinburgh, a brilliant young Aberdonian doctor named Donald Campbell, and severely injured his wife and fourteen other persons. On the same day, a similar explosion at Victoria Station wounded five of the railway staff. Agents of the I.R.A. collecting money in America told a reporter that Dr Campbell's death was not due to any change of policy in the I.R.A. – it was an 'accident'. They claimed that the I.R.A. had had four deaths (*The Times*, 29 July).

The misguided enthusiasts responsible for these outrages had not been left to carry on their work undisturbed. At first the task of tracking them down was fairly simple, for their activities centred round I.R.A. sympathizers resident in Britain and well known to the Special Branch at Scotland Yard. Moreover, the new generation of militants showed the same naïve recklessness in the custody of documents which the old Fenian leaders had deplored more than half a century earlier, but had in fact often exhibited themselves. 'Battalion Orders', recipes for making bombs, operational plans, and revolutionary poetry were left in open drawers (in one case coded documents and the cypher were in the same drawer) apparently for the convenience of an overworked C.I.D. This was too good to last. The young recruits learnt, as the dynamitards had done in the eighties and as our British agents were to learn in the Second World War, that when one is operating in a foreign country the fewer contacts one makes with residents possibly known to the police, the longer one goes free. They learnt also that secret instructions are best conveyed orally. In certain respects these revolutionaries showed considerable aptitude for guerrilla warfare. They were hardly ever caught red-handed in planting bombs, and they successfully concealed the sources from which they obtained their explosives – no mean feat. They were possibly assisted by Irish sailors on British ships, as the dynamitards had been in the eighties, but no charge was ever made. In the concealment of 'dumps', however, they were not so fortunate.

On 29 January 1939, a great haul was made in the Edgehill district of Liverpool; over a ton of explosives, a stock of fire-arms, and a large quantity of alarm clocks with holes bored in the face were seized by the police. Numerous arrests followed, and during the months of February and March there were important trials of I.R.A. members at Manchester, Liverpool, and the Old Bailey. Following an old tradition, many of the prisoners refused to plead.

In Manchester the centre of the conspiracy proved to be

the proprietor of an Irish dance club who had brought the explosives from London under the pretext that they were beeswax for his dance floor. Orders from Headquarters in Dublin had been found at the house of one of the prisoners, including a document directing attacks on England's public services without loss of life. 'We Irish in England are in an excellent position to use this method. We are accepted as fellow countrymen and allowed to partake of the same employment' – a situation they were doing their best to destroy.

In the case of the Liverpool arsenal already mentioned, the purchase of the materials was traced to a group of men tried in London on 23 March. The leader here had also run a 'social club' and had evidently been a main agent in the purchase of supplies for the I.R.A. Other prisoners had borne the proud titles of 'O.C. Great Britain' and 'O.C. London' respectively. This trial was not devoid of human interest. One prisoner refused to come into Court, and when brought forcibly lay down on the floor of the dock. Mr Justice Humphreys regarded him with cold indifference. 'Let him stand, sit, lie, as he prefers,' he ordered. The man got up instantly. Later on, the defence was put up that the potassium chlorate found on the premises had been bought for the innocent purpose of making throat lozenges. Dr Roche Lynch, the analyst, appearing for the Crown, made a rapid calculation on an envelope and informed the Court that the amount seized would, at medical doses, make seventeen million lozenges. Even the prisoners laughed.

Sometimes a premature explosion would reveal a hideout where I.R.A. experts, graduates of the training schools in Eire, were manufacturing their bombs. Other arrests in Scotland and Wales picked up some of the men engaged in hunting for gelignite in mines and quarries. It is impossible not to sympathize with two unfortunate men caught by a detective with some gelignite in a suitcase, who tumbled over each other to explain that they were no politicians but only burglars carrying their normal professional equipment.

By the beginning of July it was plain that the campaign

was drifting into the rapids and that a disaster was only a question of time. The most optimistic supporter of the I.R.A. must have found it hard to discover evidence that their cause was making headway. To the British people the explosions had no relevance whatever to the dispute over the border, and only served to make rational discussion impossible. The I.R.A. performances in the field were not so inefficient considering the lack of first-rate personnel, but the leadership was proving very defective. Sean Russell had sailed for the United States on 8 April to explain a campaign which certainly needed a lot of explanation – and to collect the necessary funds. His place as Chief of Staff had been taken by Stephen Hayes, the Adjutant-General of the I.R.A., who has made no secret of his inadequacy for such a testing responsibility as the conduct of a war against Britain, an enterprise from which greater men have shrunk. The difficulties on his side of the campaign were enhanced by the passage on 14 June of the Offences against the State Act – Eire, a very comprehensive measure directed against the I.R.A. Clause I ran as follows :

Every person who usurps or unlawfully exercises any function of government whether by setting-up, maintaining or taking part in any way in a body of persons purporting to be a government or by any other action or conduct whatsoever shall be guilty of felony and shall be liable on conviction thereof to suffer penal servitude for a term not exceeding ten years or to imprisonment for a term not exceeding two years.

Part III dealt with 'unlawful organizations', and gave the Government power to issue a Suppression Order against any body which 'advocates or encourages or attempts the procuring by force, violence or other unconstitutional means of an alteration in the constitution', or, 'raises or maintains a military or armed force'. In July 1939 the Irish Republican Army was declared an unlawful organization.

It would have been contrary to all traditions of rebellion that such a measure should have an immediate effect, and the dreary toll of outrages continued.

In July both the Irish and English legislatures made further efforts in their own ways to call a halt to violence. In the Seanad, on 26 July, the Taoiseach (Mr de Valera) stated,

No one can have any doubt as to the result of the campaign in England, and no one can think that this government has any sympathy with it. I would like to make an appeal to the people who are carrying on the campaign to ask them how they could hope to have a decision by means of this kind. ... I do believe that a number of them are animated by high ideals but I believe that they are misreading Irish history and making no allowance for changed circumstances.

The approach of the British House of Commons, which represented those at the receiving end of the bombs, was naturally somewhat more robust. There was universal support, irrespective of party, for the Home Secretary (Sir Samuel Hoare) when he rose to introduce the Prevention of Violence (Temporary Provisions) Bill on 23 July. He told the House that up to that date sixty-six members of the I.R.A. had been convicted; and 1,500 sticks of gelignite, 1,000 detonators, two tons of potassium chlorate, a quantity of ferrous oxide, seven gallons of sulphuric acid, and four hundredweights of aluminium powder had been seized. Loss had been incurred by at least 1,000 men and women. There had been a total of 127 terrorist outrages, fifty-seven in London and seventy in the provinces. By this time, he added, the conspirators had learnt to leave no written instructions but flitted from place to place.

The Bill gave the Home Secretary powers to issue Expulsion Orders against suspected persons resident in England and to issue 'Prohibition Orders' against suspicious characters attempting to enter the country. The police were given authority to arrest persons suspected of complicity in the explosions without warrant and to detain them for five days. Search warrants could be issued by the Home Secretary, or in the case of grave emergency by police officers not below the rank of superintendent. On 28 July the Bill became law.

Even the threat of new police powers had been sufficient to produce what *The Times* called a 'great exodus of Irishmen' from England. By 3 August, thirty-nine Expulsion Orders had been issued. The ports could now be more efficiently watched for the entry of new recruits, and those already engaged in active operations in England (Sean Russell had put their numbers at 500 to 1,000) could be drastically thinned out. The war clouds over the Continent were growing more ominous from day to day and it was essential that the nation should have no distraction from its immense task of self-defence.

*

The story of the fatal episode at Coventry may be said to begin with the arrival in that town of a young plasterer's labourer who called himself James Richards, his real name being M'Cormac or McCormick. He had been born in Tullamore, West Meath, on 7 July 1910, but had recently lived in the market town of Mullingar. So far as any record goes, Richards's career had been blameless. In the fourteen years since he left school he had held various semi-skilled jobs, broken by much unemployment. It was the impression of everyone he met after his arrest that by character and capacity he was fit for better things than fate had brought him. For such a likeable fellow he was curiously friendless and had neither wife nor sweetheart. Physically he was well-built, medium-sized, unremarkable except for a curious fixed stare which may have been due to the tension under which he had lived for many months.

It is not known when Richards joined the I.R.A., but apparently he was sent to England early in the campaign and operated in London and the Midlands. About the end of May he was posted to Coventry as an 'operating officer', and at the beginning of June took lodgings in the house of a fellow Irishman, one Joseph Hewitt, who was then living in Meadow Street. Hewitt and his wife Mary had come over from Belfast some three years before this date. He was a heavy, quiet man, like Richards a semi-skilled labourer, and in that summer of 1939 he was working as a 'tinner' or tin-smith's mate. A permanent member of his household was his mother-in-law, Mrs Brigid O'Hara, a plump, rather garrulous lady who earned her keep by minding the house, the lodgers, and the Hewitts' adored fifteen-month-old baby while Mary Hewitt took a job as a shop assistant. Unemployment was then rife in Northern Ireland, and various other members of the large O'Hara clan crossed the seas from time to time to find work or enjoy a holiday under Hewitt's roof. It should be added that they were a non-political family, and no suspicion attached to any of them in the events that followed.

On 12 June the whole household migrated to 25 Clara Street, taking Richards with them. Whatever the Hewitts then knew or did not know of Richards's antecedents, they must have thought him a queer sort of lodger. He had plenty of ready money but no job, and although he had registered at the Employment Exchange, he never attempted to get work. He got up late, went to the pictures, hung about the house of entertainment which was the favourite meeting-place of Coventry Irish, and played games with his landlord in the evenings. This rather demoralizing sort of idleness (combined with incessant nervous strain) is the inevitable lot of the man 'on his keeping', as the Gaelic phrase runs, in any country at any time, and cannot be charged to personal defects in Richards's character.

About the middle of July a new factor entered into the situation. The hint that fresh powers were to be conferred on the police alarmed the Coventry I.R.A. about the safety of their usual hiding places for munitions.* Hoping that the Clara Street house was not under suspicion and would escape search, Richards began to store potassium chlorate, and possibly other explosives, in this most unsuitable spot.

* Their fears were justified. Some 400 premises in the city were searched within a few days of the passage of the Prevention of Violence Act.

Clara Street is a short thoroughfare of small brick villas in a good residential district of Coventry. Its quiet, respectable air made it in some ways an excellent cover for illicit activities, but the houses are too much under the neighbours' eyes, especially at the rear, for the comfort of conspirators. Even the least inquisitive neighbour could not fail to note when visitors called and what was going on in the back garden. Most serious consideration of all for a conspirator instructed not to endanger life, an explosion in one house would inevitably wreck the whole closely packed street.

Richards kept his potassium chlorate in a suitcase, but as this method of storage was obviously unsafe he formed the crazy notion of making a dump in the tiny cupboard under the stairs. On 31 July he was seen by a neighbour digging in the floor of the cupboard; about the same time other neighbours noticed that concrete was being mixed in the back garden. This development was too much for Mrs Hewitt, who was no fool and had already been badly upset when she noticed Richards distributing white powder out of his suitcase to mysterious callers. Now she realized that the family would be living on a munition dump, and she begged her husband to get rid of this dangerous lodger. But Hewitt's only reply (as he indeed admitted at his trial) was to retort that he took full responsibility for what went on in the house. She could take the baby back to Belfast if she wished – he had a good job and would stay in Coventry. The poor woman was only too well aware that he might get no work in Belfast and that not only she but her mother and child were dependent on him. Very understandably she smothered her feelings and stayed. But she had won her point over the pit in the cupboard : it was never used.

On Sunday, 13 August, occurred an event which probably modified the projected bomb plot considerably. At 4.45 that afternoon a small shed (six feet by eight feet) on a Corporation allotment in Coventry blew up with an explosion which covered the ground for twenty yards around with a whitish powder (subsequently found to be potassium chloride), fragments of rubber balloons, and particles of metal. Two men had been seen by witnesses entering the shed a few minutes before the explosion, and then running away just before it happened. They had a narrow shave.

Police inquiries showed that the shed had been erected in the previous March by the tenant of the allotment, an Irish labourer who had since returned to Belfast. It had been frequented in the evenings by young men not known to the other allotment holders : whatever these lads came for it was not to grow vegetables, for the ground remained untended. After the trial in December a witness identified Richards as one of the men seen running from the shed. It was then learnt that this had been one of the major explosive stores for the local I.R.A. Richards had, with incredible carelessness, dropped a lighted cigarette on a floor littered with grains of potassium chlorate, which of course caught fire immediately. He had tried to stamp out the flames, scorching his clothes in the process – but the result we already know.

It is possible that the destruction of this store was responsible for the entry on the scene of the second main character in the drama, Peter Barnes. He was a more recent visitor from Ireland than Richards, a country-bred labourer of thirty-two, who left his home in Banagher, Co. Offaly, and his job as a 'steamraiser' under the County Council, to assist the campaign for the abolition of the Border. As we know from the letter found on him at his arrest, he had had a depressing time since his arrival. The men he had been ordered to contact were not there, probably because the police were too active. He took a gloomy view of the future of his work. Having at last met a friend in Liverpool, he had made his way to London and had taken lodgings near his fiancée, a girl from his native town. Barnes's part in the organization was to convey explosives from central sources of supply (principally Liverpool and Glasgow) to operating officers who were concerned in the manufacture of the bombs and in the staging of explosions.

On the afternoon of Monday, 21 August, Barnes had

come to Clara Street on a preliminary visit, as a good revolutionary should, to make certain before he brought the 'stuff' that his colleagues were still at large and that he was not just walking into a police trap. After one talk, Richards asked Mrs O'Hara to go out and buy a suitcase for Barnes, for which she was to get a receipt. While she was out, her daughter was dispatched to purchase two flour-sacks; apparently nothing was said about a receipt this time, but Mrs Hewitt asked for one of her own accord as she thought the price charged for the sacks (2s.) rather high. The suitcase brought back by Mrs O'Hara was approved by the two men; the flour-sacks were rejected as being too coarse-meshed to hold the potassium chlorate for which they were required. So Mrs Hewitt, this time accompanied by her mother, returned to 'Celia's' the cake shop where the sacks had been bought, and got the florin back. The receipt was not returned; it was picked up by Barnes, who took it, together with the receipt for the suitcase and the suitcase itself, back to London, to his ultimate undoing.

Next day, Tuesday, 22 August, the conspiracy advanced a stage further. Richards and another man called at the shop of the Halford Cycle Company in Smithford Street and while Richards waited outside the other man bought a carrier cycle costing £5 19s. 6d. The purchaser, who gave a name and address which subsequently proved to be false, paid £5 down and said he would bring the balance and remove the cycle within a few days. About the identity of this man there is some doubt. One of the shop assistants recognized him subsequently as Barnes, but there is good evidence that Barnes was in London all that day. Mrs O'Hara and her daughter said he was an acquaintance of theirs named Dominic Adams, a well-known citizen of the Six Counties; Richards refused to say who he was, but denied absolutely that he was Barnes. In one of his few incautious replies under cross-examination he let slip the significant statement that the stranger was in a position to give him orders.

Wednesday was a blank day, but on Thursday, 24 August,

the fatal stream of events moved rapidly forward. In the morning there appeared at Clara Street a 'strange man', whose identity was most carefully concealed by all the witnesses. He brought with him tools, with which he worked in the front sitting-room – and again in the evening he reappeared on the same mysterious errand. About seven that night, Barnes arrived from London, this time equipped with a 'most wicked sort of luggage' – a suitcase containing a parcel of white powder. After Barnes had left, the women took the baby out in the perambulator and, not for the first time, walked the streets until about 11 o'clock. This curious habit, which had been commented on by the neighbours, might well be explained by a desire to keep the child away as long as possible from the 'perilous stuff'.

The next day, Friday the 25th, the plot matured. The Hewitts went to work early as usual, and later the 'strange man' reappeared and finished making the bomb. How far Richard actually assisted him can never be known. He said he only looked on, but it is a fact that a setter for an alarm clock was found in his pocket on his arrest, and there was no clock it would fit in the house. There was no reason why a man in Richards's position in the I.R.A. should be squeamish about making or helping to make a bomb.

At about ten past twelve the bomb was parcelled up, and at about the half-hour Richards left to fetch the cycle from Halford's shop. He returned at ten past one and left the cycle in a 'jetty' (as Coventry oddly calls its back lanes) behind the house. There the 'strange man' picked it up, put the bomb in the carrier, and started on his grim journey. He had been getting rather fussed, understandably enough, for the bomb was set for 2.30 and it must be nerve-racking work to ride behind a bomb nearing its time limit. In Broadgate, he left the cycle resting on the kerb in front of a stationary motorcar standing before Astley's shop – and then he disappears out of history, for though his identity was well known to many people, most regrettably he was never caught.

At 2.32 the bomb exploded with the dreadful results

described at the trial. There had been some forty explosions in Coventry since the I.R.A. campaign began, but nothing like this. Friday is market-day in the town and the streets were thronged – those orders 'not to endanger life' cannot have weighed heavily on the man who could leave a five-pound bomb ticking in a congested thoroughfare like Broadgate. It was fortunate that the casualties were confined to five people killed, twelve gravely injured, and forty or more slightly injured. The dead were James Clay, an old man of eighty-one, John Corbett Arnott, a schoolboy of fifteen, Gwilym Rowlands aged fifty, Rex Gentle aged thirty-three, and Elsie Ansell, a girl of twenty-one who was to be married in a fortnight. One cannot attempt to estimate what these disasters meant in personal suffering to the victims and their relatives.

The first news of the tragedy reached Richards through a neighbour, and some time later Mrs O'Hara, full of lamentations, arrived home with an evening paper. He claimed at the trial that he was horrified because 'he thought he was told' that the bomb was to go off at night, and also because it was contrary to the policy of the I.R.A. to destroy human life. But it is hardly credible that if the bomb had been set for the evening it would have been dispatched in the carrier cycle at 1.30 p.m., to stand unguarded in some public place for five or six hours. It is much more likely that Richards was not being frank with the Court, and if he had really been disconcerted it was more by the *place* than by the time of the explosion.* It may be surmised that the bomb was intended for some public building, say the Coventry electric plant, and that the rider (having perhaps had experience of the uncertain quality of the I.R.A. clocks) had abandoned his ship in mid-channel. If this supposition is correct, the essential character of the plot is in no way affected; an explosion even in an electricity plant is highly dangerous to life.

The explosion in Broadgate had left a clue in the shape

* One of the Paddington bombs seized the same day was also timed for 2.30 p.m.

of the fragments of the carrier cycle which had been partially blown under the car standing behind it. The number was fortunately preserved, and by evening the police had secured from Halford's staff a description of the men who had bought the cycle. Further clues came through a roundabout route involving Peter Barnes and his London associates.

It happened that the 'terrible insistent routine' of which the S Plan speaks had put Scotland Yard on the trail of a London plot to discharge three five-pound bombs similar to the Coventry bomb on that same unlucky Friday. For this purpose Barnes had supplied explosives to a group of men living in Leinster Gardens, Paddington, near his own lodgings. About midday on 25 August the men were caught carrying the bombs downstairs to load on to three vehicles, a carrier cycle and two tricycles. After an exciting chase over the roofs the police arrested four of the band. It was subsequently discovered that the bombs were destined for New Scotland Yard, Westminster Abbey, and the Bank of England.

When Barnes returned to his rooms in Westbourne Terrace at 8 o'clock that night he found Detective-Sergeant Hughes waiting for him with the alarming greeting, 'We are police officers and have reason to suspect you of being in possession of explosives and being concerned in causing an explosion in Coventry.' The police had already found in Barnes's room three packets of a heavily scented 'shampoo powder', which later proved to be potassium chlorate, and traces of aluminium powder. When he was arrested a fateful letter to 'Jim Kelly – Parnell Square, Dublin' was discovered in his jacket. This unlucky document had been written after his visit to Coventry the previous night (Thursday), and instead of putting it into a pillar-box he had, like many a man before and since, posted it into his pocket. The results were fatal to him, for the contents left no doubt whatever of the nature of his activities or of his foreknowledge of the Coventry explosion. The letter read as follows :

Dear Jim, I am sure your wondering why I did not write but I no you will understand how things are. I am still here in London I am very lookey so far T.G. I got it very hard after coming over. I did not meet the man I was to meet. He was gone so I had to go to Liverpool the next day and I did not meet any one there either so I was a week and did not meet one. I was nearly mad so then I met one and he told me all was gone but himself so I had to fix up things for myself. We got over a few then and got things fixed up what I am on. I go from one place to the other and bring the S— believe me it is hard but I gotway well so far. I am after coming back from Coventry tonight 11.30 so by the time you get this the Papers should have some news. Of course I do not when I will be picked up. I am sure you can see by the papers how things are. I would not advise you to think of coming over now and it looks very like War. It may be good for us. Some of the boys think that any way but dont no. Well Jim I do hope your kid is all right by now and I do hope you were able to get the money fixed up alright as I am all right for money so far. If I dont luse them after this job then I will be fixed very bad for its cost me 5/6 a night for bed and breakfast and I grub out for the day, so it cost some to stay here. Well Jim I will say no more this time for it is very late and I have to be out very erely in the morning. You no I cant give you any address. Tell Kenny I was taken for him and I could not write to him. I may be going over to Dublin soon. There may be a letter there from you. I got one the day I left so no more. I will write you agen if I can. I would love to get a letter from you but I cant. So cheers for R from your old pal. Dixon.

'That is just a letter I wrote to a friend,' Barnes said to Sergeant Hughes in that fatal 'moment of truth' which catches some prisoners when they feel a policeman's hand on their shoulder. No amount of subsequent fabrication could cancel out that simple avowal.

The nearby flat in which Sarah Keane, Barnes's most unhappy and loyal fiancée, lived with her married brother and his wife, was also searched, and amongst other papers he had given her for safe keeping were found the Coventry receipts for the suitcase and the sacks. It is remarkable that the internal discipline of the I.R.A. should have required receipts for trivial expenses incurred on duty. These documents are an administrative convenience which underground bodies notoriously cannot afford; they are much too useful to police and to prosecuting counsel, as this case proved. It is fair to Barnes to say that he had not asked for the receipt for the payment for the flour-sacks and had possibly picked it up with the other by mistake.

On Monday, 28 August, the next blow fell. All Coventry was buzzing like a swarm of angry bees, and over the week-end inhabitants of Clara Street had reported stories of suspicious sights and sounds at No 25. At midday, Chief Inspector Boneham of the Coventry City Police, Detective-Inspector Barnes of the Special Branch, and other officers descended on the little house. They had already followed up the clue of the receipts. The shop assistant who had sold the suitcase could give no help; but, by a piece of bad luck for the plotters, pretty blue-eyed Celia at the cake shop was one of those people who never forget a customer. She had given the police a description which exactly fitted Mrs O'Hara, and that lady readily admitted the transaction. The first link was forged between Clara Street and the London bomb-setters.

The search of the Hewitts' house by the team of experienced police officers revealed much that was suggestive of I.R.A. sympathies, but nothing very definite. However, there was enough material to justify the detention of all the inhabitants of the house at the police station that night. They were allowed out on bail until 5 September while deportation orders were applied for. Later in the week the Forensic Laboratory experts reported that traces of potassium chlorate were present in a suitcase found in the Clara Street coal-shed. The pieces of the jigsaw puzzle were now fitting together and the pattern of the conspiracy was becoming clearer. On Saturday, 2 September, the two Hewitts, Mrs O'Hara, and Richards were all arrested under the Prevention of Violence (Temporary Provisions) Act, and kept in custody (Barnes was, of course, already under detention in London).

On the two following days, the women, who were appalled, as well they might be, at the consequences of the mischief concocted under their roof, made statements concerning many of the events leading up to the explosion. On Tuesday, 5 September, all four prisoners were charged with offences under the Explosive Substances Act, 1883. But they had an even greater ordeal to undergo. After careful consideration the Public Prosecutor decided on 27 September that the facts justified a charge of murder against all five prisoners. Their cases were committed for trial to the Birmingham Assizes to be held in December 1939.

*

The four-day trial, which opened on 11 December 1939, at the Birmingham Assizes, attracted national interest. England was still in the doldrums of the 'phoney war', and no blitz had yet arrived to blunt the memory of the Coventry explosion. In any case the appearance of five prisoners in the dock on a murder charge was sufficiently unusual to make the trial noteworthy in criminal history. An I.R.A. directive (of which a copy had been seized early in the campaign) giving authority for the employment of legal aid for members charged with a capital offence had either been ignored or withdrawn, for all the prisoners were defended as 'poor persons', a task involving heavy responsibility on the solicitors and counsel who appeared for them. The counsel who led for the prosecution was, as it happened, a co-religionist, and by birth a fellow-countryman of the prisoners, and was well acquainted with the political and historical background of the tragic story. Behind the scenes stood the impressive figure of Chief Inspector Parker of New Scotland Yard, whose highly competent preparation of the case for the Crown made the trial a model for students of Court procedure. There were no loose ends; the tangled story was ready to be unfolded systematically before the jury; every point the defence could make had been anticipated and investigated.

From the legal point of view, the questions raised proved to be less complicated than was feared at first. The points at issue – all very familiar to lawyers – were explained lucidly by counsel for the prosecution in his opening, by the judge in his summing-up, and were further discussed before the Court of Criminal Appeal. They need only be summarized here for the benefit of the general reader.

Was the charge against the accused properly one of murder? This was hotly disputed by the prisoners' friends in Eire, but so clearly is the principle established that even Mr Woods of the Eire Bar could not challenge the indictment when he appeared for the prisoners in the Court of Criminal Appeal. There were two well-known legal doctrines involved. The one is embodied in the ancient rule of English law that where a person committing a felony does an act which is known to be dangerous to life, and life is in fact lost, that is murder, even if the death were undesigned. Clearly, causing or aiding or abetting the explosion of a five-pound bomb in a place frequented by human beings, whether that place was a main street or an electricity plant, whether the bomb was set for 2.30 or 6.30, was just such a felony – and as we know, life had in fact been lost.

The other doctrine is the well-established rule of 'common purpose'. If two or more persons agree to commit a dangerous felony which results in a death, all the persons in the combination or conspiracy are guilty of murder, not only the person who did the actual killing.

These rules had been applied to Irish prisoners taken in arms before (as in the Manchester trial of 1867), but they were not, as is sometimes supposed, maliciously invented to subdue political demonstrators; they are part of the ordinary practice of the English Courts. Cases in point such as *R. v. Browne and Kennedy*, in 1928, and the Antiquis murder, have greatly impressed the public with a sense of the value of the rule of 'common purpose' in preserving the lives of peaceful citizens. The same principles apply whether the motive of the killing, or the felony which led up to it, is lust or gain or the redressing of a political grievance; there is no special law for ideological homicide. Whether there should be greater clemency shown to prisoners convicted of murder who have acted from political motives, or whether in their case capital punishment is justifiable at all, are quite other matters. To the law as it stands is probably due, at least in part, the extreme rarity of fatal incidents in political and industrial disputes in this country : every member of a group has a common interest in discouraging dangerous violence on the part of any other member, and the leaders have the strongest incentive of all. Established authority is not the only gainer from this situation; the horrid sequence of death from political or mob violence, legal penalties, and reprisals, leaves permanent scars on all parties.

The next point requiring decision was whether the five prisoners should be tried together. This is a matter entirely for the discretion of the presiding judge, and in this case Mr Justice Singleton decided on a joint trial for a reason admirable in its cogency and simplicity – 'in order that (the jury) should have the evidence of each one in considering the whole case'. There is much to be said in favour of joint trials in cases where there is no grave reason to the contrary. It is surely one of the main objects of criminal procedure to ensure that the jury should learn *what actually happened*, and in the case of a concerted crime it may be impossible to give a complete picture if the prisoners are tried separately, and an attempt to do so merely leads to much overlapping and waste of time. Separate trials may also lead to anomalies such as grossly inconsistent verdicts, to harsher treatment of less guilty partners in crime, to acquittal of the more guilty.

Where prisoners are tried together it is of course necessary to take special precautions to ensure that the case of no one of them is prejudiced. The jury has to be warned that the charge must be fully proved against each. Further, it is the rule that 'if a statement has been made by one of the accused, it is evidence only against the person who makes it, and not against the other accused'. This often-quoted proposition is perhaps more satisfying to the lawyer than to the ordinary citizen. It suggests that juries unlike other human beings have a mechanism in their brains which enables them to know and not to know something at one and the same time. All it really means, as the judge told the Birmingham Court, is that juries 'should not accept as [evidence] against someone something that is said behind his back', a much more understandable maxim and one confirmed by observation in daily life. It is difficult to see what other principle Courts could adopt in cases where statements have been made by prisoners charged together with others. To insist that in such circumstances there should *never* be a joint trial would be clumsy and possibly unfair : statements can be helpful as well as detrimental to fellow-prisoners.

In this trial the question of admission of statements, which threatened at one time to loom very large (for those made by the women were of great importance), turned out to be of merely academic interest, for all the prisoners went into the witness-box and repeated the substance of what they had said. Their statements were thus placed on the same level as their other evidence, and became subject to cross-examination by the counsel for the other prisoners.

There had been very little newspaper publicity about the prisoners, and when they filed into the dock their stories and personalities were quite unknown to the jury and the public. The two women prisoners gained immediate sympathy, only deepened by their testimonies in the witness-box – so evident was it that both had been unwillingly caught up in a current of events too strong for them. Poor flustered Mrs O'Hara was a 'bad witness', in the technical sense of the term, if ever there was one, creating as she did all sorts of unnecessary mystifications by her failure to understand simple questions. She had lived almost wholly among Irish folk during her three years in Coventry and was, one gathers, still puzzled by English accents and turns of speech. Her daughter, Mary Hewitt, gave the impression of a more stable, simpler character, wholly taken up with interests of her husband and baby, from whom she had now been separated for three months. It had been her one comfort that the relatives in Belfast had repaid Hewitt's past services with a most affectionate welcome to the child. It is only fair to both women to say that many of the discrepancies and contradictions in their evidence were obviously due to natural lapses of memory in people not accustomed to precise observation. How could they be sure whether Barnes, or Richards, had said this or that, or whether there were two men or three in the back kitchen at a particular moment? Their evidence, it may be held, did Barnes and Richards no substantial harm, for these men were amply convicted by their own deeds and out of their own mouths. For Joseph Hewitt, that very negative character, the joint trial was pure gain, for the two women's testimony clearly encouraged the jury to take a wide view of the rather generous and unquestioning hospitality he had afforded his fellow-countrymen. For Barnes, of all the prisoners, the ordeal must have been the most terrible. He could not have failed to realize ever since his arrest that he was in great peril, and for this situation he seems to have been wholly unprepared. He had no notion that in acting as a conveyor of high explosives he was endangering his own life at the hands of the law, nor that he could in any way be held responsible for the fatal effects produced by the 'stuff' he peddled. It did not help at all that he sought to explain away the overwhelming facts against him – the letter to Jim Kelly, the Coventry receipts, his identification by a Mrs Grose in Clara Street, the explosives found in his room – by stories which Mr Justice Singleton charitably described as 'foolish'.

It is common observation that revolutionary activities do not bring out the best in every man, and the evidence shows that Barnes was apparently one of those unfortunates who have mistaken their vocation. A man can only give what he has got. In personal relationships he had evidently shown excellent qualities. He had nursed his dying wife devotedly through a long illness; much love from family and friends surrounded him up to his last moments.

There was something more than pity in the emotions aroused by his comrade in misfortune, James Richards. In the long weeks of waiting for his trial his unwavering attitude had been, 'We know what's coming to us and we can take it.' He could and did. He knew quite well that his part in the conspiracy resulting in the destruction of five human beings could not be covered by an apology however sincere. Moreover, there is every reason to believe from his own statements that if the I.R.A. had ordered him to continue organizing similar plots with similar risks to life, he would have done so.

Even those who find Richards's point of view morally perverted – or wholly incomprehensible – must be struck by the watchful loyalty he showed throughout the trial to the Hewitts (on whom his presence had brought such appalling misfortune), to his own organization, and to his comrades in the conspiracy who were not before the Court. There is dignity as well as courage in many of his replies under cross-examination. That last brief speech from the dock is in the ancient tradition of Irish patriotism.

I wish to state, my lord, before you pass sentence of death on me, I wish to thank sincerely the gentlemen who defended me during my trial and I wish to state that the part I took in three explosions since I came to England I have done for a just cause. As a soldier of the Irish Republican Army I am not afraid to die, as I am doing it for a just cause. I say in conclusion, God bless Ireland and God bless the men who have fought and died for her. Thank you, my lord.

Cheerful indifference to a capital charge and the ensuing sentence is not necessarily a sign of virtue, as every prison official knows. It may be present in the vilest of men; it may betoken brutish stupidity, or that obscure sickness of mind we label 'psychopathic personality'. In James Richards it appeared to spring genuinely from the satisfaction a man feels at having performed what he believes to be his highest duty.

The jury returned a verdict of guilty against Barnes and Richards. Joseph Hewitt, his wife Mary, and Mrs O'Hara were acquitted. The convicted men lodged an appeal, which was dismissed on 23 January 1940. They were executed on 7 February at Winston Green Prison. Hewitt was charged the day before at the Old Bailey with causing an explosion and having explosive substances. No evidence was led and he was discharged.

John George Haigh

· 1949 ·

BY

LORD DUNBOYNE

FOR several years two elderly ladies, a Mrs Lane and a Mrs Durand-Deacon, had been living under the same roof in South Kensington at the Onslow Court Hotel. They had become close friends and, while they were in London, saw each other daily. One evening Mrs Lane happened to notice that the table where her friend was accustomed to dine was unoccupied. The date was Friday, 18 February 1949.

Next morning another resident, whom Mrs Lane knew only as a nodding acquaintance, asked her if Mrs Durand-Deacon was ill. He explained that Mrs Durand-Deacon had arranged to accompany him to Sussex on the previous day, but that she had not kept the appointment to meet him. Mrs Lane, mystified, went upstairs and had a word with the chamber-maid. It appeared Mrs Durand-Deacon had been out all night and had not yet returned.

Mrs Lane's anxiety was mounting and on the following morning, when the same solicitous inquirer came to the breakfast table and again asked her if she had any news, she roundly replied that she intended to report her friend's disappearance to the police. The inquirer appeared to be pondering the remark. Not long after breakfast he resumed the conversation : in the lounge, he approached Mrs Lane with the suggestion that he himself should drive her to the police station. Had Mrs Lane known all she subsequently learned about her escort, she would scarcely have accepted his invitation as readily as she did. As it was, she arrived with him that Sunday afternoon at the Chelsea Police

Station where they together reported that Mrs Durand-Deacon had been missing since the afternoon of the preceding Friday.

Following the report, a police-sergeant called, as a routine measure, at the Onslow Court Hotel to talk with those who knew Mrs Durand-Deacon, and who might assist in tracing her. Presumably because it was a woman who was reported missing, it was a woman police-sergeant who performed the duty of instituting inquiries. Among those interviewed was the manageress of the hotel, who gave the sergeant an unfavourable account of the resident who had accompanied Mrs Lane to the police station. A check was soon made and it was discovered from the Criminal Records Office at the Yard that the man in question, a Mr John George Haigh, who seemed so plausible, had more than once been convicted for crimes of dishonesty. Could it be that his greed or need for money had induced him to commit a yet more serious crime?

On Monday afternoon he was interviewed by two detective-inspectors at his hotel. 'I will tell you all about it,' he said, and proceeded to make a statement in which he professed to have no notion of Mrs Durand-Deacon's whereabouts. Three days later, when the police again interviewed him at his hotel, he made a substantially similar statement.

Meanwhile the search was extended. A description and picture of the missing person was issued to the Press, and journalists flocked to the Onslow Court Hotel. They had many questions to ask Haigh, who glibly recounted the same story he had told Mrs Lane and the police. Far from avoiding publicity, he gave a sort of mass Press conference to some of the leading crime reporters of the country. The occasion has been described by Stanley Firmin in his book, *Crime Man*.

Haigh stressed his hope that Mrs Durand-Deacon would be discovered safe and sound. 'I am just as anxious as you or anyone else is on that score,' he said with apparent sincerity.

But crime reporters are blunt and persistent men. Looking Haigh straight in the eye, one of them suddenly remarked: 'I think you ought to know, Mr Haigh, there are rumours that you have a criminal record.' Thereafter, Haigh could have been left in no doubt that he was under suspicion. But he did not end the interview or even protest at the disconcerting innuendo. 'Let us skip that,' he said with a wave of the arm. 'We are talking of Mrs Durand-Deacon. Now ...' and he went on calmly with some fresh graphic observation about the missing widow and her personal characteristics.

Already the West Sussex Constabulary were on the scent. Their assistance was enlisted because Haigh, in his statements to the Chelsea Police, described himself as a director of Hurstlea Products Ltd in Crawley. The representation he volunteered was no doubt calculated to give an impression of respectability. It proved to be not quite true, but it was a signpost to many a clue.

By 23 February, the police had interviewed Mr Jones, the managing director of Hurstlea Products Ltd. It transpired that Haigh sometimes used the storehouse of the firm, ostensibly for experimental work, and that he had recently told Mr Jones he was engaged on 'a conversion job' there. The storehouse was a brick-built two-storey shed, situated in Giles Yard which was surrounded by a six-foot-high fence, flanking Leopold Road on the outskirts of Crawley. The firm used it for the purpose of housing steel and other surplus materials which could not conveniently be accommodated at the main business premises in West Street, Crawley. The storehouse was secured by mortice and padlock; and, so far as Mr Jones knew, Haigh still had the keys in his possession. To obtain entry, Detective-Sergeant Heslin, accompanied by Mr Jones, forced the padlock with a steel bar on 26 February.

Inside were discovered certain articles which, at first sight, might have seemed to have been used for 'the conversion job' to which Haigh had alluded; but a revolver and various papers, including a receipt of a firm of cleaners in Reigate for a Persian lamb coat, were also found. The coat was collected the next day from Reigate by the police and soon identified as Mrs Durand-Deacon's. Two days later, to crown suspicions, came the news that, on the very day after Mrs Durand-Deacon had disappeared, her jewellery had been brought by Haigh to Messrs Bull's jewellery shop in Horsham for valuation and sale.

Divisional Detective-Inspector Symes thereupon advised Detective-Inspector Webb by telephone to bring Haigh without delay to the Chelsea Police Station. Consequently, at 4.15 p.m. outside the Onslow Court Hotel, Haigh was waylaid in his car and requested by Inspector Webb to come with him at once. 'Certainly,' replied Haigh obligingly, 'I will do anything to help you, as you know.'

In the police station, where eight days previously he had reported Mrs Durand-Deacon missing, Haigh continued to affect a detached air. Sitting in an easy chair in the office of the Divisional Detective-Inspector, he nonchalantly smoked, read newspapers, and dozed. At 6 p.m. he was given a cup of tea, but no mention was yet made of the nature of the inquiry for which he was required. So prompt had his arrival at the Station been, that two or three hours elapsed before the police were ready to question him.

At 7.30 p.m. the fateful interview started, in the course of which Haigh's miscalculated manoeuvres could scarcely have done more than they did to queer any line of defence open to him. His answers to the questions, which were very properly put to him by the police, started with a damning lie about his visits to Horsham. He then shifted his ground. Saying he saw the police knew what they were talking about, he admitted that the Persian lamb coat, which had been recovered from the cleaners in Reigate, was Mrs Durand-Deacon's, and that he had sold her jewellery in Horsham. Both admissions contradicted his previous explanations.

Then when asked, under caution, how he had come by the property and where the missing person was, he invented the excuse that it was all a long story of blackmail. Again he prevaricated, asking how he stood about implicating others.

'What you have to say is entirely a matter for you,' said Inspector Symes, who at that point left the room for ten minutes.

Alone with Inspector Webb, Haigh turned to him as man to man and asked him frankly what were the chances of anyone being released from the criminal lunatic asylum at Broadmoor. As a matter of fact, the chances were about 150 to 1 against being released; but it was an ill-judged question, which might have told heavily against Haigh at his trial, appearing as it did to betray an ulterior motive for what he was about to add. The Inspector correctly declined to discuss the matter at all.

'Well,' continued Haigh, 'if I told you the truth, you would not believe me; it sounds too fantastic for belief.' Presumably in the hope of a comfortable sojourn at Broadmoor, he now decided to make a quite astonishing admission. A second time that evening he was cautioned that he need say nothing, but out came the bombshell.

'I will tell you all about it,' he said. 'Mrs Durand-Deacon no longer exists. She has disappeared completely and no trace of her can ever be found again. I have destroyed her with acid. You will find the sludge which remains at Leopold Road. Every trace has gone.' An equally revealing afterthought followed : 'How can you prove murder if there is no body?'

No corpse, no conviction. It was a simple maxim and a naïve interpretation of the law as regards murder. Haigh seems to have clung to the idea tenaciously. It is said to have been the topic of a discussion he had had with his fellow-prisoners when he was serving one of his earlier sentences: after various methods of disposing of the remains of a victim had been discussed. Haigh aired his pet theory that murder could not be proved without a corpse 'because, you see,' he explained, 'there would then be no *corpus delicti*'. This highbrow *ratio decidendi* was met with the contempt it deserved. His companions chuckled and Haigh was thereafter known in that prison by the nickname of 'Old Corpus Delicti'.

The story rings true. It was Haigh's delight to pose as a cleverjack; but his little learning was a dangerous thing and led him astray more than once. So it had on this occasion.

Corpus delicti, the phrase which had caught his fancy, does not mean the corpse of the crime, as he may have supposed. It is a legal term of art, connoting the body, in the sense of the gist or essence, of the offence; it comprises the fact that criminal agency has caused, for instance, burning, in a case of arson, or death in that of murder.

The prosecution is of course obliged to prove the *corpus delicti*, to prove the gist of the offence charged. But what Haigh did not appreciate was that the prosecution, when alleging murder, might still be able to prove the *corpus delicti*, even if no trace of the victim's body were found; there might still be sufficient evidence, either direct or circumstantial, of the victim's death and of its cause to enable the prosecution to prove the murderer's guilt, as in the case of James Camb, who disposed of his victim through a porthole at sea. A mere confession without other evidence would probably not suffice; if the accused could be convicted for murder on his own word alone, there would be no sufficient reason why the alleged victim might not subsequently reappear alive. But suppose a confession were made which contained a full description of the circumstances of the crime. How much less difficult might it be then to obtain from other sources the necessary amount of evidence for the prosecution to prove its case. Assistance of such a suicidal nature could scarcely be expected by the police from a prisoner before trial. Yet such was precisely the extent to which Haigh now chose to cooperate.

As soon as Haigh had told Inspector Webb of Mrs Durand-Deacon's fate, Superintendent Barratt, who was in charge of the inquiry, and Inspector Symes were called into the room. Haigh was again cautioned, and he then dictated to Inspector Symes a statement which, apart from an interval for tea and bread and cheese, took two and a half hours to reduce to writing. In it Haigh announced for the first time that he had shot Mrs Durand-Deacon. In considerable detail he described not only the circumstances of the crime, but the pecuniary profit of £111 10s. it had brought him. He went further, and, with reference to various documents bearing the names of McSwan and Henderson which had been found, stated that he had killed the five people concerned and on each occasion drunk their blood, as in the case of Mrs Durand-Deacon.

Haigh did not finish the statement until the small hours of the morning of 1 March. He was thereafter detained in custody where he earned the reputation of being a well-behaved and almost elegant guest. He was given every facility compatible with police regulations, and made no complaint. On 2 March, Haigh was taken from London to Horsham Police Station, where he was charged by Detective-Superintendent Eagle with the murder of Mrs Durand-Deacon. He was cautioned and said, 'I have nothing to say.'

On the same day he was brought before the Horsham Magistrates' Court on the charge. Local interest in the case was ablaze, and at the doors of the court police reinforcements were required to restrain a surge of over two hundred people. Only formal evidence of arrest was given that day, and Haigh was remanded in custody. On 4 March, at Haigh's own request, Inspector Webb visited him in Lewes Prison. First satisfying himself that the police were convinced of the truth of his long statement of 28 February, Haigh told the Inspector he considered it 'timely' to mention three other people, a woman from Hammersmith, a youth from Kensington, and a girl from Eastbourne, who, he said, completed the list of his victims, totalling nine in all. The statement was taken down and signed by Haigh in the presence of witnesses, but no charge of murdering anyone other than Mrs Durand-Deacon was ever made against him.

*

The case of the Acid Bath Murder, as it came to be known, captivated the imagination. All the ingredients of a horrifying mystery were being unearthed, and to the popular mind the case was a *cause célèbre* of the first order. In its essentials, the capital charge, formulated against Haigh, was not difficult to appreciate: a financially embarrassed man of apparent charm had ingratiated himself with a widow of some wealth, inveigled her into a death trap, dissolved her body in sulphuric acid, and reported her to the police as a missing person. Then, when cornered, the accused heaped horror upon horror, fully describing the crime without any trace of remorse and coolly claiming to have killed eight other human beings and to have drunk their blood.

There was nothing exceptional about a murder for money; most murders are done for money. Nor had Haigh shown particular originality in his method of disposing of his victim's remains. For when Haigh was but a choir-boy in Wakefield, Georges Sarret in France was buying a bath and a hundred litres of sulphuric acid, which he thought 'might come in useful sometime'; Sarret's crime conformed to precisely the same pattern as Haigh's: the French acid bath murderer successively shot two people on 19 August 1925, unquestionably for gain, and decomposed their corpses in an acid bath. The preliminary inquiry in the French case, however, lasted two years, instead of one month. Sarret was tried at Aix-en-Provence in October 1933, and found guilty of the double murder and of another one in addition. There were no extenuating circumstances and therefore, in accordance with the Code Napoléon, he was ordered to be guillotined in public. Haigh may have read of the case and borrowed the Frenchman's ideas; at any rate, Haigh was not the first known acid bath murderer.

Nor did Haigh by any means hold the record for multiple murders. There was in recent time Silvester Matuska who, in October 1931, admitted to having murdered no fewer than twenty-seven people in railway crashes he engineered on the continent of Europe. It was the same number of victims whom Marcel Petiot, guillotined in 1946, was convicted of having murdered; and the French police suspected

him of having slaughtered thirty-four more. Bloch of
Chicago killed twenty-six, Harman of Hanover twenty-four,
and Landru of Gambais eleven. The Bluebeard of Gambais
may indeed have killed hundreds more than the eleven for
whose deaths he was convicted. Parenthetically, a remarkable set of coincidences is presented by the affinity between
Landru and Haigh : both were witty; both were once
choristers; both once worked in garages; both avoided
military service; both were previously sentenced for swind-
ling; both kept incriminating diaries; both used the medium
of newspaper advertisements to obtain introductions to
several of their respective victims; both were multiple murderers, apparently for gain; and both were convicted of
murder, after trials which at the time aroused more world-
wide interest and attracted more publicity than any of the
others here mentioned.

Yet, besides hitting the headlines, the case of Haigh
possessed features of more durable interest. Their interest
was not confined to the legal profession, but spread to Fleet
Street, Scotland Yard, and Harley Street. Briefly, the significant aspects of the case may be classified as fourfold.

First, before the trial but not unconnected with it, a
national newspaper fell foul of the law. On 4 March 1949,
the *Daily Mirror* published matter relating to a person on a
criminal charge, which prompted Haigh's counsel to move in
the King's Bench Divisional Court for writs of attachment;
the contempt of Court complained of was ultimately penal-
ized on an unprecedented scale, the newspaper being fined
£10,000 and costs and the editor sent to prison for three
months.

Second, unusual difficulties confronted those engaged on
the work of detecting the murder. In the last fifty years, only
three other murderers in Britain are believed to have presented comparable problems of identifying the remains of
the victim.

Third, the proceedings for contempt of Court were not the
only aspects of the case which were rich in legal interest : the

case of Haigh evoked a judicial pronouncement on the proper 'venue' of the trial; the case was tried before a great criminal judge, assisted by eminent counsel; it possibly provided a legal precedent of the recognition of the anomaly of paranoia as a 'mental disease' under the M'Naghten Rules; and, as will be shown, the course the trial took was peculiar in the extreme.

Fourth and finally, the mental condition of Haigh was of unusual psychological interest. The notoriety of his trial was justified, not so much by the number he claimed to have killed or by the method he adopted to conceal his crimes, as by his extraordinary claim to have drunk his victims' blood. No other reported case seems traceable to suggest that a murderer drank, or claimed to have drunk, the blood of the murdered, as an end in itself unassociated with any sexual perversion.

The volume of work which the investigation of Haigh's crime necessitated was enormous. The evidence which was ultimately heard in court disclosed, as in most cases, only a fraction of the painstaking detective work and probative research accomplished behind the scenes.

Thanks to Mrs Lane's insistence on reporting to the police that her friend was missing, the machinery of the law was set in motion. In its initial stages, the ensuing inquiry was, for the police, very much a matter of everyday routine. Information of the missing person was automatically sent to all police stations in the Metropolitan Area by teleprinter, and to every police force in Britain by means of the current edition of the *Police Gazette*. In addition, it was the normal practice, on receipt of such a report, for an officer trained for the purpose to interview anyone who might assist the search. The police are frequently notified that someone or other is missing. In the following year, for instance, which was a fairly average one, no less than 1,059 persons were so reported to the Metropolitan Police Force alone; and only a small proportion of the disappearances were found to be the result of foul play. It reflects all the more credit on the police that, in the present case, having received such a familiar report, they should have promptly entertained the possibility of murder and focused their attention on Haigh.

On returning to the Chelsea Police Station, Woman Police-Sergeant Lambourne apprised Inspector Symes of the result of her inquiries at the Onslow Court Hotel. The Inspector consequently telephoned Scotland Yard who, within the hour, replied with the information that Haigh had a criminal record. From that moment, Haigh was a marked man.

It was, however, not possible to arrest him without grounds for a reasonable suspicion that he had committed the felony for which he was to be charged. Although suspicions, based on mere intuition and previous convictions, were not enough, one wonders why the police did not arrest Haigh immediately after they found such damning evidence against him in the storehouse at Crawley. No doubt there were good reasons for waiting another two days. Certainly, in the interim, important evidence, which implicated Haigh in the sale of Mrs Durand-Deacon's jewellery, was obtained with the aid of publicity in the Press.

Criticism, from the highest motives, is directed at the Press for devoting space to unsavoury matter relating to crime. But it is not always appreciated that the very publications which the respectable citizen is inclined to deprecate may prove of material assistance to the police in their task of bringing the criminal to book. If, for instance, on 20 December 1914, the Sunday Press had not chosen to report an Islington inquest in some detail, George Joseph Smith would probably have gone free to murder more than three of his brides in the bath. Again, it was in consequence of Press publicity about the disappearance of Mrs Durand-Deacon that on 28 February 1949 Messrs Bull of Horsham informed the police of jewellery which had been brought to their shop the day after Mrs Durand-Deacon had vanished. On receipt of the information, Inspector Symes collected the jewellery and was able to have it identified as Mrs Durand-Deacon's by her sister. Moreover, the customer who had sold it had signed his name as 'J. McLean' of '32 St George's Drive, s w' – a neighbourhood, incidentally, with which Haigh had grown familiar as a firewatcher in the recent war – and he had been recognized by the jeweller's assistant as one who had been to the shop before and given his name as J. G. Haigh.

Delaying no longer, the police then pounced. Haigh was brought to the Chelsea Police Station, only a few minutes before he was about to deliver to his solicitors the illuminating files which were found, neatly packed, in his hotel room. On 1 March, the day when Haigh, in the small hours of the morning at Chelsea Police Station, completed the dramatic statement in which he claimed that no trace of Mrs Durand-Deacon could ever be found, the Chief Constable of the West Sussex Constabulary applied to New Scotland Yard for the assistance of a Chief-Inspector and a pathologist.

Chief-Inspector Mahon consequently assumed charge of the investigations and went with Dr Keith Simpson and Inspector Symes to Giles Yard in Crawley, the site of the storehouse which Sergeant Heslin and Mr Jones had entered three days before. For the following detailed account of the subsequent investigations, I am chiefly indebted to Dr Keith Simpson.

The majority of the human remains were found in that part of the yard which lay opposite the storehouse on the other side of the track that ran down the length of the yard. The ground was rough and covered with debris with which a large quantity of greasy sludge lay mixed to a depth of some three to four inches over an area of some six feet by four feet. Immediate search resulted in two important discoveries. One was an object about the size of a cherry and looking very like the small stones among which it lay. On close inspection it was found to have polished facets which revealed it was no mineral pebble, but a human gall-stone. Secondly, embedded in a thick charred greasy substance, there lay several masses of eroded bone, the largest of which proved to be the greater part of a left foot.

Some 475 lb. of a conglomeration of grease and earth was lifted carefully by shovel and removed in boxes to New Scotland Yard for laboratory examination and sieving.

A forty-gallon green painted drum, fitted with a lid, lay on end near by. Its interior was soiled with the same greasy substance, and a hairpin was stuck in the grease at the bottom of the drum.

Inside the storehouse were found the various articles which Sergeant Heslin and Mr Jones had seen there three days previously. The very finely spattered blood-stains which adhered to the whitewashed wall were photographed and carefully detached for laboratory examination : the precipitin test showed them to be human, although there was insufficient material for grouping tests.

On the laboratory bench at New Scotland Yard, the 475 lb. of dirty, greasy, oily residue, soaked into the pebbly earth, was exposed on steel trays and patiently searched during the following three days. From the conglomeration were recovered :

1. a mass of some 28 lb. of yellow greasy substance resembling melted body fat;
2. three faceted gall-stones of human type;
3. part of a left foot, eroded by acid;
4. eighteen fragments of human bone, all corroded by acid to a varying degree;
5. intact full upper and lower dentures;
6. the handle of a red plastic bag;
7. a lipstick container.

Further laboratory investigations were at once made. A whole series of gall-stones, known to be of human origin, were examined and their precise constitution determined. They were compared with specimens of other mammalian gall-stones, from all of which the human gall-stones showed a constant difference in composition. Furthermore, a laboratory test procured a positive precipitin reaction, with human antiserum, from a portion of one of the three gall-stones found at Crawley, thus leaving no doubt that they were of human origin.

The eighteen fragments of partly eroded bone were identified as :

1. a left ankle pivot bone (talus);
2. a small part of the centre of the right foot, with attached ligamentous tissues;
3. a right heel bone (os calcis);
4. a right ankle pivot bone (talus);
5. three lengths of eroded long bone cortex, probably thigh bone (femur);
6. parts of each hip-girdle (pelvic bone);
7. a fragment of the hip crest (pelvic wing);
8. a small piece of the lower spinal column, together with eroded parts of two intervertebral discs;
9. seven further small fragments, too far eroded for exact anatomical definition.

All these residual fragments were eroded by a strongly acid fluid, and sharply distinguishable from certain animal bones which, though lying in the same soil surface, showed no such changes. In view of the discoveries which supported Haigh's statement that he had dissolved Mrs Durand-Deacon in sulphuric acid, elaborate tests on dead animals and amputated human limbs were conducted to confirm that concentrated sulphuric acid would rapidly decompose a human body. The process of dissolution would probably be complete within twenty-four to forty-eight hours. No external source of heat would be necessary because the inter-action of the acid with the water present in the tissues would be sufficient to raise the temperature to a degree at which dissolution would be accelerated. Fatty material from the body would resist even hot sulphuric acid, and would, there-fore, be expected ultimately to form a solid scum. The sub-stitution of fresh acid would eventually hasten the process, although the addition of cold acid to a sludge containing only partly eroded bone might at first leave the bone still incompletely attacked.

Plastics, on the other hand, would offer far greater resistance to acid; and acrylic resin would scarcely be dissolved by strong sulphuric acid in less than three weeks. The full set of artificial dentures which had been found at Crawley were made of acrylic resin, and, being still completely intact, were of prime importance.

Mrs Durand-Deacon had experienced considerable gum shrinkage which had necessitated numerous visits to the dentist, and her dental surgeon, Miss Mayo, had kept a plaster cast of the patient's upper and lower jaw. Miss Mayo was consequently able to swear that she had, in 1947, supplied Mrs Durand-Deacon with those dentures found at Crawley. Her identification of the owner of the dentures was thus as conclusive as the evidence of the meticulous dental witness in the case of the Baptist Church Cellar Murder.

In fact, probably only in that case and two others had comparable problems of reconstructing and identifying the remains of the victim been presented in twentieth-century Britain. The sludge and slime at Crawley yielded evidence analogous in its scantiness to the small pieces of flesh found buried in Crippen's cellar, or to the butchered maggot-infested portions of human corpses collected near the ravine when Mrs Ruxton and her maid were missing : or to the burned torso discovered in the cellar of the Baptist Church some fifteen months after Mrs Dobkin had last been seen alive. But the amount of material available in the Ruxton case was overwhelmingly more abundant than in that of Haigh, while in the cases of both Crippen and of Dobkin the remains had to some extent been preserved by lime, instead of having been eroded by acid.

As has been seen, the body of Mrs Durand-Deacon was identified from her fragmentary remains, although Haigh evidently believed no trace of her could be found. Moreover, within only a month from the time of Haigh's arrest, the case for the prosecution was ready for trial. It was a triumph

of scientific detection. To the police, both uniformed and
C.I.D. alike, congratulations are justly due; and the thanks
of the community for being rid of the monstrous Haigh are
none the less due to that little old lady who in her wisdom
one Sunday afternoon conscientiously reported at the Chelsea Police Station that Mrs Durand-Deacon was missing.

*

On the application of the prosecution, Haigh was remanded
from week to week on four occasions until, on 1 April, evidence was called. That morning the Horsham Town Hall
was bathed in sunshine when E. G. Robey opened the case
on behalf of the Director of Public Prosecutions, before ten
Sussex magistrates, three of whom were women.

Haigh, looking spruce in a green Lovat suit, seemed to
relish the limelight of infamy and to be wholly oblivious to
the gravity of his position. He sat in court, taking copious
notes and ever alert to indulge in his usual lighthearted
banter.

For instance, when Robey, in the course of his duty as
prosecuting counsel, grasped a stirrup-pump to show the
exhibit to the Court and stung his hand on some remnants
of sulphuric acid, Haigh was as highly amused by the incident as if Robey's father, that great comedian, had done
a music-hall turn. He barely had the sense of occasion not
to yell, 'April fool.'

Again, when Sergeant Heslin described in evidence his
forcible entry into the Crawley storehouse, Haigh scribbled
a note to his legal advisers, facetiously suggesting that the
sergeant be prosecuted for 'breaking and entering'.

In the two-day hearing before the magistrates, G. R. F.
Morris, who appeared for the defence, called no evidence.
The prosecution agreed with him not to disclose those passages of Haigh's statements to the police which referred
either to the drinking of blood or to the killing of others than
Mrs Durand-Deacon. Methodically, Robey called thirty-
three witnesses whose evidence dovetailed to present the

prosecution's case of a carefully premeditated murder by Haigh for gain. Their depositions, recorded by a noiseless typewriter, were similar in substance to the evidence given for the prosecution at the trial itself. A brief chronology of the facts which emerged from that mosaic of evidence may assist the reader. The cumulative effect which such details, given on oath from a witness-box, would have upon the minds of a jury will thus be seen to advantage. For the facts speak eloquently for themselves when recited baldly in the form of a diary :

Monday, 14 February: Haigh is in debt. His unsecured overdraft at the bank amounts to £83 5s. 10d. He owes his London hotel nearly £50; and recently when he made some effort to pay his hotel bill his cheque was not met.

Mrs Durand-Deacon is seen by a Mrs Birin at lunch in the hotel to converse with Haigh and to show him a box of plastic fingernails.

Tuesday, 15 February: Haigh goes to Crawley where he asks Mr Davies, a local engineer, to fetch some acid from London. Haigh also sees Mr Jones, the managing director of Hurstlea Products Ltd, who listens without enthusiasm to Haigh's suggestion about manufacturing artificial fingernails. Before returning to London, Haigh borrows from Mr Jones fifty £1 notes to be repaid not later than the end of the week.

Wednesday, 16 February: With a wad of notes Haigh pays Mrs Kirkwood, the head book-keeper of his London hotel, the £50 due on his bill. Again in Crawley, Haigh takes to the storehouse the engineer, Mr Davies, whom yesterday he has asked to collect the acid. There, Mr Davies sees three carboys, all partly full of acid, one of which he takes with him after it has been emptied into the others. At the same time, Haigh gives Mr Davies two £1 notes, with a written order to Messrs White, the London manufacturing chemists, for one carboy of commercial sulphuric acid in 'confirmation of telephonic order to Mr Brown today'.

Thursday, 17 February: Mr Brown, the sales manager of

Messrs White, receives the 'telephonic order' from Haigh for a carboy, containing some ten gallons of acid, which Mr Davies duly collects. When depositing it at the storehouse in Crawley, Mr Davies sees no such green drum as Exhibit 25 there.

Late in the afternoon Haigh brings to Mr Jones in Crawley a new stirrup-pump, the foot of which he wants sawn off. Knowing Haigh's inability to handle tools, Mr Jones extracts two rivets so that the instrument's foot is severed. (The removal of the foot would make it possible to insert the pump in the narrow neck of a carboy, so as to pump out acid into a drum which would hold a human corpse.)

Earlier in the afternoon, Haigh has acquired a drum from Messrs Blagden of Barking. Mr Savage, a clerk of that firm, can prove that Haigh has taken, and signed a receipt for, an ordinary forty-gallon black drum, while Mr Sheterline, the firm's works manager, knows that between 3 and 4 p.m. a person, answering to Haigh's description, has exchanged a black drum for a green one, specially prepared to resist corrosive acids.

Friday, 18 February: Haigh spends an hour or so of the morning with Mr Jones in Crawley, helping to move some steel from the storehouse. Between 1.30 and 2.30 p.m., he is seen by Mrs Kirkwood at his hotel in London. Mrs Durand-Deacon is seen in the same hotel, not only coming from the dining-room at lunch time, but at about 2.15 p.m., carrying the handbag which is found a month later outside the storehouse in Crawley. At the George Hotel in Crawley, a woman in a Persian lamb coat, whom the witness is able to identify from a photo as Mrs Durand-Deacon, is seen shortly after 4 p.m. by the hotel book-keeper, Miss Caplan. Mrs Durand-Deacon and Haigh visit respectively the ladies' and gentlemen's cloakrooms and then drive away in his car. She is not seen again.

At about 4.45 p.m., Haigh tells Mr Jones in West Street, Crawley, that he thinks the person he was bringing to see about the artificial fingernails has not turned up. At a few minutes to 6 p.m., a Mr Baker is parking his van near the storehouse and, by the light of his head-lamps, sees a man going to and from the storehouse and a car close by. An hour later, Haigh is in Crawley, eating an egg on toast at Ye Olde Ancient Priors Restaurant and chatting lightheartedly with Mr Outram, the proprietor. Haigh is still in Crawley at 9.30 p.m. when Miss Caplan sees him entering the dining-room of the George Hotel.

Saturday, 19 February: At breakfast in his London hotel, Haigh tells Mrs Lane that Mrs Durand-Deacon has not accompanied him to Sussex the previous day.

Later in the morning Haigh is in Horsham trying to have some jewellery valued at Messrs Bull's. Mr Gegg, who attends to him, is able to recognize Haigh from a previous visit. On learning the licensed appraiser is out, Haigh says he will call again.

Another firm of jewellers, Messrs Barrett in Putney High Street, buys from Haigh, for £10, a wrist watch, later identified as Mrs Durand-Deacon's by her sister Miss Fargus. Although Haigh gives a false name and address, he can be identified by Mr Richmond, the manager, as the vendor of the watch.

In Reigate, the same day, Mrs Marriott, an assistant of a firm of cleaners, receives for cleaning a Persian lamb coat, later identified as Mrs Durand-Deacon's by Mrs Lane. An expert furrier is able to give his opinion in evidence that the coat is in fact Persian lamb and that its second-hand value is about £50. On it, Dr Holden of the Metropolitan Police Laboratory subsequently finds a small patch of human blood. The receipt which Mrs Marriott gives for it is, next week, found in the Crawley storehouse.

At about 4 p.m. Mr Jones sees Haigh in Crawley.

Sunday, 20 February: Haigh and Mrs Lane together report at the Chelsea Police Station that Mrs Durand-Deacon is missing.

Repayment of Haigh's debt of £50 to Mr Jones is now overdue.

Monday, 21 February: Apparently from Chichester, Haigh telephones Mr Jones about the debt. At 6 p.m. in Crawley, Haigh promises Mr Jones repayment on the morrow.

Continuing to profess ignorance of Mrs Durand-Deacon's whereabouts, Haigh, at his London hotel, makes his statement.

A Mr Banbury is cleaning and pressing Mrs Durand-Deacon's coat at Reigate, while jewellery, later identified as hers by her sister Miss Fargus, is brought by Haigh to Messrs Bull in Horsham for valuation. They pay him. Giving a false name and address, Haigh pays 25s. for the valuation in which the jewellery has been assessed at £131 14s.

Tuesday, 22 February: The jewellery, valued yesterday by Messrs Bull, is, at about 12.45 p.m., sold to them by Haigh in Horsham at £100, towards which Mr Gegg pays Haigh sixty £1 notes forthwith.

In Crawley just before lunch, Haigh has promised to repay Mr Jones the £50 overdue. At 2 p.m. in Crawley, Haigh partly discharges his debt by paying Mr Jones £36.

Wednesday, 23 February: Haigh makes his fourth visit in five days to Messrs Bull of Horsham, where he is paid in notes the further £40 for the jewellery they have bought from him.

£5 is paid into Haigh's account at his bank in Crawley, reducing his overdraft to some £78. In Crawley just before lunch, Haigh calls on Mr Jones, as he did yesterday. But, today, Mr Jones says he has been interviewed by the police and begs Haigh, if he is in trouble, to stay away from the works.

Thursday, 24 February: Haigh, professing the same ignorance and innocence as he did last Sunday and Monday, makes another similar statement at his London hotel to Inspector Symes.

Saturday, 26 February: Sergeant Heslin, with Mr Jones, forces entry into the storehouse. Inside are found three carboys, the footless stirrup-pump, a mackintosh, a pair of rubber gloves, a gas-mask case, and a rubber apron while in the far corner of the room are a square leather case and an attaché case.

When later analysed by Dr Turfitt of the Metropolitan Police Laboratory, samples of the contents of two of the carboys are revealed to be a commercial grade of concentrated sulphuric acid. Dr Turfitt further discovers that the stirrup-pump is corroded, both inside and out, by the sulphuric acid and that sulphuric acid and animal fat are upon the mackintosh, gloves, and apron. In addition, Dr Holden is able to certify that human bloodstains are upon the gas-mask case and, though mingled with fibres of beechwood, also upon the apron.

The square case, on examination, is found to contain a revolver in a holster, together with eight rounds of ammunition in an envelope. The revolver, which according to one witness is a Webley, and to another an Enfield, has in the opinion of the firearms expert, Dr Turfitt, been recently fired.

In the attaché case is a receipt from the cleaner at Reigate for the Persian lamb coat.

Sunday, 27 February: Inspector Symes, with Sergeant Heslin, retrieves the Persian lamb coat from the cleaners at Reigate.

Monday, 28 February: Inspector Symes, in the hotel room which Mrs Durand-Deacon occupied, finds a bag in a workbasket. Portions of fabric in the bag are found to match exactly with patches on the bottom of the coat and on a repaired part of its left sleeve.

Inspector Symes then goes to Horsham and collects from Messrs Bull the jewellery which Haigh has sold them.

At about 4.30 p.m., Inspector Webb, on instructions, brings Haigh to Chelsea Police Station, where Haigh makes his long confession, and is detained in custody.

Tuesday, 1 March: Chief-Inspector Mahon, accompanied by Dr Keith Simpson, goes to Crawley and takes charge of those exhibits already specified by Sergeant Heslin as having been seen in the storehouse last Saturday. Inspector Mahon also takes charge of the following articles : two pieces of red cellophane, a roll of cotton wool, a respirator in the gas-mask case, a hairpin found in the green drum which Mr Sheterline of Messrs Blagden exchanged on 17 February for a black one, and the green drum itself; also, a bucket, a wooden rod, and an oval base and part of handle of a plastic handbag, all of which when examined by Dr Turfitt bear traces of sulphuric acid and animal fat. Corrosion discovered at one end of the wooden rod suggests to Dr Holden that it has been used for stirring acid. If it had been wiped on the rubber apron in the process of stirring, the rod would have shed the beech-wood fibres found on the apron.

Specks of blood on the whitewashed walls of the storehouse are removed and preserved by Inspector Mahon for examination by Dr Holden, who considers them to be recently formed human blood-stains.

Outside the storehouse, Inspector Mahon supervises the lifting of the soil, which is placed in five large wooden boxes to be examined by experts. Dr Turfitt finds it contains sulphuric acid, a high percentage of animal fat, and a certain amount of calcium and phosphate, the chief mineral constituents of bone. Dr Keith Simpson extricates from the sieved soil a red plastic handbag handle, a lipstick container cap, human gall-stones, a number of bony parts, and most important of all a full set of upper and lower dentures. In his opinion the bony parts represent one human body, while their fragile nature and a partly preserved bone of the hip girdle indicate that they are the bones of an elderly woman. The dentures are those supplied to Mrs Durand-Deacon in 1947 by her dentist, Miss Mayo, and identity of the remains is thereby clinched.

In Haigh's hotel room in London, Inspector Symes surprisingly finds the famous shopping list which is proved to be in Haigh's handwriting by his bank manager and which itemizes several of the exhibits found in the storehouse in Crawley.

In turn, Inspector Mahon finds in Haigh's room a bundle of papers referring to the families of McSwan and Henderson, and a blue shirt, a cuff of which has, in the opinion of Dr Holden, been recently stained with human blood, as has the whitewashed wall of the storehouse.

Wednesday, 2 March: Inspector Mahon finds a blood-stained penknife in the cubby-hole of Haigh's car.

At Horsham Police Station, Superintendent Eagle charges Haigh with the murder of Mrs Durand-Deacon.

Friday, 4 March: Haigh makes a written statement to Inspector Webb claiming to have killed three others in addition to the six persons named in his statement of last Monday night.

Tuesday, 8 March: Sergeant Heslin finds a chain, identified as Mrs Durand-Deacon's by her sister, and an attaché case key at Buxted where Haigh said they were to be found.

Saturday, 19 March: Outside the storehouse, Sergeant Appleton finds a handbag which, together with the handle found by Dr Simpson, and the base and other handle by Inspector Mahon, forms such a bag as that which Mrs Lane saw Mrs Durand-Deacon carrying at lunch-time on 18 February. In it Sergeant Appleton finds a lady's round metal powder compact and a silver pencil, identified as Mrs Durand-Deacon's by her sister, Miss Fargus.

The foregoing facts, uncontroverted and incontrovertible, which leave out of account the numerous details contained in the various statements made by the prisoner himself to the police, give some measure of the strength of the evidence presented by the prosecution against Haigh on 1 and 2 April before the examining justices and on 18 and 19 July before the trial judge and jury.

Towards the close of the proceedings before the examining justices at Horsham, Haigh's counsel suggested that the case be tried in London. In the circumstances, the application was not unreasonable, although the crime was alleged to have occurred in Sussex and the venue provided by Common Law for the trial was consequently the Sussex County

Assizes at Lewes; the next Lewes Assizes were not due to open until more than three months later, and, moreover, most of the witnesses in Haigh's case came from London. With a view to expediting trial and saving expense, the Horsham Magistrates were, in the circumstances, empowered by Section 14 of the Criminal Justice Act of 1925 to commit Haigh's case to some convenient assizes, other than those for the locality of the crime.

Robey, for the prosecution, tendered no objection to such a course being taken; but he did warn the magistrates: 'Sometimes a strong line has been taken at the Central Criminal Court when a committal from the country has taken place. The judge has said that the trial could not take place there and has sent it back to the country assizes,' on the principle that London jurors should not be burdened with country cases.

Nevertheless the request of Haigh's counsel was acceded to and Haigh was committed to be tried at the Central Criminal Court (the 'Old Bailey').

Haigh's defence was, however, not ready for trial at the prescribed time. Consequently, on 27 April, Maxwell Fyfe, with Morris, made an application at the Old Bailey on behalf of Haigh to have the trial postponed. The Crown was represented by Anthony Hawke, the Senior Treasury Counsel. It appeared that Haigh's defence was not completed because some scientific evidence was awaited, and the 'Red Judge' was invited to defer the trial until the following sessions at the Old Bailey. If the application had been granted, the trial could still have been heard at the Old Bailey some six weeks earlier than it would have been at the next Lewes Assizes. Yet Mr Justice Humphreys adopted the 'strong line' to which Robey at Horsham had prophetically adverted and, in no uncertain terms, the case was remitted to Lewes.

Since the judge had become a member of the Central Criminal Court Bar Mess as long ago as 1891, he spoke from a long personal knowledge of the practice obtaining at the

Old Bailey. If quoted here, the views he expressed may be conveniently accessible to magistrates and others concerned:

In this case an application is made to postpone the trial of this capital offence until the next session of this Court. My view is that that application can only be made as a result of a misunderstanding of the law as it exists, and the practice as it often exists. This case has nothing whatever to do with the Central Criminal Court. The indictment before me is a charge of murder in Sussex. Haigh was arrested at Horsham on 2 March, nearly two months ago. The duty of the Horsham Magistrates was to commit Haigh for trial at the next Sussex Assizes. This person is entitled in law to a jury of Sussex persons. This Court is here ready to try him. But now, at the last moment, the Court is told that the defence, which must have said from committal that they were perfectly willing, are not ready for trial. This case is a Sussex case and should be tried in Sussex, as is the normal course, and now application is made that I should postpone it until the next sitting of this Court.

Unfortunately, of late years the idea has grown up that the Central Criminal Court is a sort of dumping ground for criminal trials from all over the country. There still remains in this country the law of venue. This man is entitled to be tried by a Sussex jury, which is a very strong reason for not sending the case away from the proper court to some alien court.

I hope that in future if such applications are made they will be refused. The Central Criminal Court remains the Assize Court for the City of London and the Central Criminal Court district, as defined in the Act of Parliament – the County of Middlesex, the administrative County of London and certain parts of Essex, Kent, and Surrey. It has its own jurisdiction, its own work – and very, very heavy work. There is no ground for acting or thinking that it should be used as a place where any serious case committed for trial might be sent to be tried although the jurors of London have nothing to do with the case. It is for that reason that I cannot accede to the application to postpone the case until the next session of the Central Criminal Court. The application would have been granted as a matter of course if it had been an ordinary Central Criminal Court case, but it is not.

I refuse that application. But in order that the accused may not say that he has been required to stand his trial at a time when he was not ready, in the rather vague language of counsel, because he was discussing with some eminent scientists some question or other, I will remit this case to be tried at the place which it should never have left. The indictment will go back to the County of Sussex and he will be tried at the next Lewes Assizes.

It was already known that Mr Justice Humphreys was due to preside at the next Lewes Assizes; so, in his eighty-second year, another notable British trial was to be added to the long list of those in which he had participated.

*

The trial took place in Lewes, at the County Hall. Built in 1812, pursuant to an Act of Parliament, and substantially altered in 1894, it had superseded the Old Town Hall and Sessions House which in the eighteenth century occupied the middle of the High Street. In the Assize Court there, on the morning of 18 July 1949, Mr Justice Humphreys in scarlet robes took his appointed place beneath the royal coat of arms. Near him on the rostrum sat the High Sheriff, whose arrival had been heralded in accordance with custom by a fanfare of trumpets. His duty it would be to employ the services of the executioner, should Haigh be sentenced to death.

In black gowns, an imposing array of counsel were there to take part in the trial. Not only Eric Neve and Gerald Howard but also the Attorney-General himself all appeared for the Crown. Seldom, unless the administration of poison has been alleged, has the Attorney-General been personally engaged in a murder trial. But the trial of Haigh proved a departure from the general practice, as have certain other exceptional cases, such as those of Fox, of Holt, of Light, and of Rutherford.

The Attorney-General, Sir Hartley Shawcross, in his early days at the Liverpool Bar, had been a pupil of Sir David Maxwell Fyfe. Both subsequently won fame at the Bar, at the Nazi Nuremberg Trial, and in Parliament. While Shaw-cross was now leading the prosecution in his capacity as representative of the public interest and chief law officer of the Crown, Maxwell Fyfe was burdened with the unenviable responsibility of defending Haigh. 'I'm very glad,' wrote Haigh, 'to see that we have got old Maxy. He's no fool. It was a little doubtful whether we should, owing to his being tied up with the Australian Bank Appeal.' Second string for the defence was G. R. F. Morris, who, being a member of the Western Circuit, was also 'going special' : he had represented Haigh throughout the initial proceedings; and, in the third place, was David Neve, son of the second silk appearing for the prosecution; as a member of the South-Eastern Circuit he was holding a 'kite brief' to enable Maxwell Fyfe and Morris to appear on an alien Circuit.

It was rumoured that Haigh had assigned a certain newspaper the copyright of anything he was to write for the Press and that he was thereby enabled to pay for his defence. The Bar Council had expressed no opinion on whether such an arrangement should be regarded as undesirable, and its propriety was never questioned in the case of Haigh. But an arrangement of a similar nature was once made on behalf of Smith for the Brides in the Bath Case, and was vetoed, as contrary to public policy, on the instructions of the Home Secretary who was then Sir John Simon, a former Attorney-General.

Thus the trial of Haigh began. On arraignment, he pleaded not guilty. To have afforded him a further opportunity of avoiding the death sentence, his insanity would no doubt have been pleaded on arraignment if it could have been honestly suggested that he was unfit to plead. But there was no reason to suppose that Haigh was incapable of understanding the proceedings. Consequently no question of his capacity to plead was raised, and after the jury had been sworn the Attorney-General rose to outline forthwith the story of the alleged crime.

Admirably arranged, concisely worded, and temperate throughout, the Attorney-General's opening of the case for the prosecution could well be commended to students of advocacy as a model of its kind. The initial advantage of having a case to present which was relatively free of complexity in itself made the merits of the speech the more transparent : none of the artifice or high-flown rhetoric, which has characterized the histrionics of prosecuting counsel in the past, was employed; yet, despite the use of an economy of words, no detail essential to the case was omitted; nor, on the other hand, did the speech contain any material allegation which was not to be supported by the evidence of a witness; and withal it was tempered by that spirit of fairness to the accused with which the administration of the criminal law in modern England has become imbued.

The case, a straightforward one of murder, so presented by the Attorney-General, was then proved to the hilt by a succession of witnesses for the prosecution. Three of them had been bound over conditionally and were not required to be in court. The power conferred on examining justices by Section 13 of the Criminal Justice Act of 1925 to bind over a witness to attend trial conditionally upon notice given to him often saves unnecessary trouble and expense; it causes no hardship to the accused, who is informed of his right to require the attendance at trial of any witness bound over and of the steps to be taken for securing the attendance of a required witness. Thus the sworn evidence of Mr Pennells the architect, of Mr Banbury the dry cleaner, and of Mr Noble the furrier, was read aloud by the Clerk of Assize because their presence at the trial was deemed unnecessary. In point of fact, not one word of the evidence of any of the witnesses for the prosecution was challenged by the defence at trial and only four of the thirty-three witnesses for the prosecution were cross-examined at all.

The tenor of the cross-examination of the witnesses for the prosecution confirmed the general expectation that the defence of insanity would be solely relied upon : first, Mr Outram, the proprietor of the restaurant at which Haigh had a meal shortly after the alleged murder, was cross-examined as to whether Haigh, when at the restaurant, was in a jocular mood. Secondly, Inspector Symes, at the request of the defence, put in evidence those passages of Haigh's statement of 28 February which referred to the killing of the McSwans and Hendersons and to the drinking of their blood by Haigh, 'as before'. It is curious, incidentally, to note that although the defence made much of Haigh's claim to have drunk his victim's blood, throughout the trial no evidence was given to the jury that Haigh had stated he had drunk the blood of Mrs Durand-Deacon. Only in relation to those other murders with which Haigh was not charged was evidence of the blood motif introduced.

The third person to be cross-examined was Inspector Webb, who was requested by the defence to produce Haigh's statement of 4 March, which referred to the killing of three more victims. Finally, Chief-Inspector Mahon was asked in cross-examination whether he had found a blood-stained penknife in Haigh's car, the implication presumably being that Haigh had used it to make an incision on the dead body so as to obtain his draught of blood.

It was when Inspector Mahon was in the witness-box that a discussion arose on a rule of evidence which, being somewhat technical, requires a word of explanation. The Attorney-General had very guardedly asked Inspector Mahon whether Haigh had profited by the murder of the McSwans or of the Hendersons. Now it is a well-known principle of British criminal jurisprudence that the defence of a prisoner should not be unnecessarily embarrassed at trial by evidence of other offences for which that prisoner is not at the time standing his trial. But, to quote the words of Lord Sumner in the case of *Thompson* in 1918, 'sometimes, for one reason or another, evidence is admissable, notwithstanding that its general character is to show that the accused had in him the makings of a criminal, for example, in proving guilty knowledge or intent or system or in rebutting an appearance of innocence, which, unexplained, the facts might wear.' Nevertheless, the greatest care is taken to exclude such evidence so obviously prejudicial to the accused, unless it is plainly necessary to prove something which is really in issue. Thus, when Inspector Mahon was asked by the prosecution whether Haigh had profited from other murders, the judge concluded that at that stage of the trial the question which had been asked was not relevant to the charge, which was confined to the alleged murder of Mrs Durand-Deacon.

By the afternoon of the first day of the trial, the prosecution was concluded, having established by a wealth of evidence that Haigh had killed Mrs Durand-Deacon on 18 February 1949, and killed her deliberately. On behalf of Haigh no attempt was made to deny the undeniable. But Maxwell Fyfe, who had already twice declared his intention of raising the defence of insanity, rose to discharge what he described as one of the most difficult tasks which anyone could have to perform. Anticipating that Dr Yellowlees was going to say that Haigh suffered from paranoia, Maxwell Fyfe sought to outline to the Court the nature and effect of that type of aberration, and to submit that Haigh was so victimized by it as to be at the time of the crime ignorant of the wrong he was doing. The speech, which was manifestly inspired by Thomas Erskine's defence of Hadfield, who, probably in order to be put to death, had fired a loaded pistol in the direction of King George III, occupied the rest of the day's hearing.

By now, the vital and only issue at the trial was whether Haigh was not responsible for his act of killing Mrs Durand-Deacon. In effect, the riddle which faced the jury was not whether Haigh had done the deed, or even whether he had done it unintentionally, but simply whether at the time of doing it he was unaware that what he was doing was wrong according to the law of the land. Like anyone else before the law, he was to be presumed responsible for his actions unless the contrary were proved. If the contrary was not proved, and *a fortiori*, if it was positively proved that Haigh knew at the time of killing Mrs Durand-Deacon that he ought not to have been doing so, then he was punishable – under the laws of the land – by death. Haigh's fate, whether it was to be execution at Wandsworth or asylum at Broadmoor, depended on the jury's answer to the question, posed by the M'Naghten Rules : Was Haigh at the time of the crime so afflicted by a disease of the mind as to be ignorant that what he was doing was wrong?

To inform the Court of Haigh's mental condition, Dr Yellowlees entered the witness-box at the beginning of the second day's hearing. His evidence was not on the level of the psychiatric evidence of, for instance, Sir Norwood East at the trial of Ronald True. It would certainly have been better for Haigh if Dr Yellowlees had not mentioned that the prisoner had previous convictions; while an inaccuracy about the number of times he had seen Haigh, owing to a typing error in the doctor's notes, gave a slapdash appearance which was not lessened by the apparent readiness of the witness to accept the truth of Haigh's unverified statements.

But the facile diversion of picking holes in the doctor's evidence and calling it all a fiasco has obscured appreciation of the underlying difficulty in which he was placed. He had thrice interviewed Haigh – on 1, 2, and 5 July. On 2 July, it struck him that Haigh's mental condition conformed startlingly with the description of the symptoms of paranoia contained in Dr Tanzi's *Text Book of Mental Diseases*. As a doctor called upon for consultation, Dr Yellowlees felt bound to express his opinion that Haigh was mentally ill. In turn, as lawyers instructed to defend the prisoner on a capital charge, Haigh's legal advisers felt bound to call Dr Yellowlees as a witness, so that his considered opinion could be placed before the court of trial.

The crux of the difficulty, however, which faced both Dr Yellowlees and the defence, was the doctor's inability to satisfy himself in all honesty that Haigh, at the time of shooting Mrs Durand-Deacon, did not know that what he was doing was wrong. The doctor was, in fact, persuaded by the defence to give evidence only on the clear understanding that he was not prepared to commit himself beyond a doubt in respect of the effect or consequences of any defect of reason in the prisoner's mind, arising from its paranoiacal structure, that is to say that he was not prepared to commit himself on the one question which mattered. The witness was veritably on the horns of a doctor's dilemma. He could not, if he was to be honest, save the life of his patient, and of course he was honest. Consequently, any advantage his evidence in chief may have brought to the defence was heavily outweighed by the extent to which his evidence on cross-examination confirmed the case for the prosecution. The Attorney-General was in duty bound to probe the validity of the doctor's assumptions and conclusions; and he did so in a cross-examination which ultimately elicited a decisive admission. Had there been no cross-examination of the doctor, the jury would have been left with a very inadequate impression of his full opinion, as may be illustrated by the juxtaposition of the two essential extracts from his evidence:

MAXWELL FYFE: Would it be right to say at once that you are not prepared to express an opinion on whether he [Haigh] knew he was doing what was wrong?

DR YELLOWLEES: That is so.

THE ATTORNEY-GENERAL (*cross-examining*): I am asking you to look at the facts and tell the jury whether there is any doubt that he must have known that, according to English law, he was preparing to do and subsequently had done something which was wrong?

DR YELLOWLEES: I will say 'Yes' to that if you say 'punishable by law' instead of 'wrong'.

THE ATTORNEY-GENERAL: Punishable by law and, therefore wrong by the law of this country?

DR YELLOWLEES: Yes, I think he knew that.

The defence had thereby collapsed. In the circumstances, it might have been expected that further evidence would have been called for the defence; otherwise the judge might have withdrawn the issue of the prisoner's insanity from the jury by reason of sheer lack of evidence: or, if that course were not taken, the prosecution might logically have been expected, with the leave of the judge, to have called rebutting evidence. But nothing of the sort happened.

At the conclusion of the evidence of Dr Yellowlees, Maxwell Fyfe called no other witness. Haigh himself was entitled under the Criminal Evidence Act of 1898 to give evidence upon his own application and there was no rule of law to stop him from doing so even after another witness for the defence. Indeed, in the Camden Town Case, Marshall Hall put the prisoner, Wood, into the box as thirteenth witness for the defence; Wood was acquitted on a capital charge, as was Lawrence in a case in which Mr Justice Jelf said to the jury: 'Had it been that this man's mouth had been shut, I do not think he could possibly have escaped at least a verdict of manslaughter.'

Now, Haigh alone knew what had been in his mind at the time of the crime; he alone could have told the jury authoritatively whether a superior force or dreams had moved him to kill and whether he drank his own urine or his victim's blood. Of course, he was to all outward appearances disastrously sane and, furthermore, the truth was not in him. The chances were that his cross-examination by the Attorney-General would have resulted in a *débâcle* and that, as a witness, Haigh would have created a fatal impression on the jury. Yet there was an outside chance that, if placed in the witness-box, the prisoner might have convinced some member of the jury that there were sufficient grounds for returning a verdict of 'Guilty, but insane'. If he failed in the attempt, he would have had nothing to lose that was not already lost. But, as it was, he continued to toy with a crossword puzzle in the dock, in silence.

Nor should the tactics of the prosecution wholly escape criticism: at the conclusion of the case for the defence after Dr Yellowlees had given evidence, it was open to the prosecution to have submitted that there was no issue of insanity to go to the jury, or to have called rebutting evidence. To have done neither seemed inconsistent.

Perhaps it was as well that the issue of insanity was not

withdrawn from the jury. To some, justice, in that event, might not have appeared to have been done. However, the very avoidance of that course suggested that there might have been some question of the prisoner's insanity for the jury to decide. If the evidence was accordingly to be deemed not to have been all one way, then surely the prosecution should have adduced some rebutting evidence. Dr Matheson, the Principal Medical Officer at Brixton Prison, was available. He was well qualified to express an opinion on the matter in issue and his evidence, invariably clear and cogent, would doubtless have been of assistance to the Court.

The Attorney-General refrained from calling any rebutting medical evidence because, in his view, the evidence for the defence was conclusive in itself that Haigh was not insane according to law. In his final speech, the Attorney-General added the explanation that he had always been taught that it was not appropriate to call witnesses about matters in regard to which no onus was laid upon you; in other words, every person is presumed to be sane until the contrary is proved and, until then, it is inappropriate for the prosecution to call witnesses as to the sanity of the accused. It is, moreover, often distasteful for the prosecution to call further evidence when the defence is concluded and can call no more witnesses in answer.

Yet the trial of Haigh, who was a public menace, was of public concern; and during it, the prosecution should have left no stone unturned. For all anyone could have divined at the time, some member of the jury, not gifted with the Attorney-General's clarity of thought, might have entertained an honest belief that the evidence of Dr Yellowlees was not conclusive in the way suggested and that Haigh was insane at law. By the course he adopted of calling no medical witness, the Attorney-General was taking a certain amount of risk. His faith in the intelligence of the jury was, however, justified by their verdict.

So counsel delivered their closing speeches and the trial proceeded inexorably to the last amen. The judge's private conviction that Haigh was sane in no way disturbed the balance of the even-handed justice of his summing-up. No reference was omitted to any material evidence which might reasonably have assisted Haigh.

The judge suggested to the jury that the accused's admission that he had killed Mrs Durand-Deacon should for the moment be disregarded, because manifestly Haigh was 'utterly and completely unreliable' – Haigh later referred to this summing-up as a masterpiece ! The judge then referred to the defence that Haigh had set up and to the great principle that no person could be punished in this country for an act which had not been done consciously. The principle was enshrined in the so-called M'Naghten Rules, the history and practical implications of which were described in considerable detail at the trial. The circumstances were such that the jury could pronounce Haigh 'Guilty but insane' only if satisfied that he had killed Mrs Durand-Deacon, and that at the time of doing so he was suffering from a disease of the mind which prevented him from knowing his action was wrong in law. As to the interpretation of the words 'disease of the mind', the judge made the following significant observation : 'It would not be very satisfactory that you should convict somebody of murder, if he was otherwise very insane, merely because the particular form of insanity is not recognized by the [medical] profession as a disease.' It was the opinion of Dr Yellowlees that Haigh was of paranoid constitution and was suffering from some of the symptoms of pure paranoia. Dr Yellowlees called paranoia a profound mental disease. But Dr Tanzi, upon whose book Dr Yellowlees relied, had categorically written that paranoia was not a true disease. So there was some question whether paranoia could be called a disease of the mind; but the judge gave Haigh the benefit of the doubt. 'Let us assume that it is a disease,' the jury were told.

As to the decisive question of Haigh's knowledge of wrong, the defence were asking the jury, as it was succinctly put in the summing-up, to say on the evidence of Dr Yellowlees

what Dr Yellowlees would not say himself. But, throwing
into the scales all that could be added in favour of the prisoner, the judge reminded the jury that they were not obliged
to endorse the opinion of any witness, however expert.

Had the Homicide Act of 1957 been in force at this time
it is possible that Sir David Maxwell Fyfe might have made
strenuous efforts to bring forward a special plea of diminished responsibility. This, if successful, would have reduced
the murder charge to one of manslaughter. But had this been
the aim, the Attorney-General would probably have called
evidence in rebuttal. It is unlikely that such a plea would
have succeeded, for the only evidence of true aberration was
that which the accused could have given, and had he gone
into the witness-box it is probable that the jury would merely
have taken the view that he was an inveterate liar and
placed no credence on what he said. The motive all through
was clearly gain, and the jury would no doubt have thought
that he was merely trying to lie his way out with incredible
stories. It is almost certain that under the new Act the result
of the trial would have been the same in the long run.

The jury took only a quarter of an hour to decide upon
their verdict. Even then the machinery of the law opened the
loophole of insanity in favour of the prisoner as widely as
propriety permitted : when formally asking the jury whether
they found the prisoner guilty or not guilty, Mr Lancaster,
the Clerk of Assize of the South-Eastern Circuit, went out of
his way to add the words : 'or do you find him guilty but
insane?' It was a curious conclusion to an exceptional trial
that one of considerable experience in criminal procedure
should, out of an abundance of caution, have so departed
from the usual practice. It did not, nor of course was it intended to, affect the verdict, which was a straight one of
Guilty. Donning the traditional black cap, the judge sentenced Haigh to death and the Bishop who was Sheriff's
Chaplain pronounced 'Amen'.

*

The setting of Haigh's early life furnishes a peculiarly improbable background for a career of crime. He came of sturdy Yorkshire stock; and no suggestion of a strain of insanity, feeble-mindedness, or mental instability is traceable in the history of his family. His grandparents were, like his parents, pious God-fearing folk. But it may be noted that his mother has sought to attribute his perverted conduct in a marked degree to the acute anxiety she suffered for three months before his birth. She had been married eleven years, and was forty years old when expecting her first and only child. Her husband was, at the time, station-foreman in the electricity works at Stamford. One day the works changed management and her husband, through no fault of his own, was displaced by a new foreman. Deprived of a sorely needed means of livelihood, in vain he daily walked many miles in search of work. He was unemployed.

To the highly principled couple, their distress was a social stigma. They were ashamed and worried and wanted no one to know that a child was to be born to them in their plight. Their shame was by no means assuaged when they were obliged to borrow money to provide for the imminent confinement. It was a crucial and cruel juncture of their lives. The dark destitute days extended into weeks and the weeks lengthened to three months before, on 24 July 1909, at Stamford, the mother was delivered of John George Haigh.

Then the horizon brightened. The father found work, first on a temporary basis, but soon at Lofthouse Colliery, near Wakefield, where he achieved the proud record of remaining in steady employment for twenty-five years, until he retired.

Every penny of the money borrowed was repaid; and, before Haigh was a year old, his parents left Stamford to live nearer the colliery. They settled in Outwood where, at their modest abode, Haigh spent the first twenty-four years of his life. Years later in prison he wrote :

The atmosphere in my home, which even now I can feel and sense with a vividness beyond words to convey, was rather like that of some monastic establishment. It had the quietness of a strange certainty. It did not belong to the world outside.

Though my parents were kind and loving, I had none of the joys, or the companionship, which small children usually have. From my earliest years my recollection is of my father saying: 'Do not,' or 'Thou shalt not.' Any form of sport or light entertainment was frowned upon, and regarded as not edifying. There was only, and always, condemnation and prohibition.

Their sect was known as the Peculiar People. Their religious beliefs were to them more important than anything else in life. They lived by precepts, and they talked in parables. It is true to say that I was nurtured on Bible stories, mostly concerned with sacrifice.

If by some mischance I did, or said, anything which my father regarded as improper, he would say: 'Do not grieve the Lord by behaving so.' And if I suggested that I wanted to go somewhere, or to meet somebody, he would say: 'It will not please the Lord.'

He was constantly preoccupied with thoughts of the Hereafter, and often wished the Lord would take him home. It was a sin to be content with this world, and there were constant reminders of its corruptness and evil.

Often I pondered my father's references to the Heavenly places, and to the 'worms that will destroy this body'. It was inevitable that I should develop an early inhibition regarding death.

So great, in fact, was my father's desire to separate himself and his family from the evil world, that he built a great wall round our garden so that no one could look in.

But it is true, also, that my parents loved me deeply, and they devoted themselves to moulding my life. Their hopes were high, and to me they remained all that is noble.

On my father's forehead is a small blue scar shaped like a distorted cross. Explaining the mark to me when I was very young, he said: 'This is the brand of Satan. I have sinned, and Satan has punished me. If ever you sin, Satan will mark you with a blue pencil likewise.'

Naturally I remarked: 'Well, mother isn't marked.' My father answered: 'No, she is an angel.'

My dismay was acute when at school this story was received with scorn. I soon dropped the idea that I must be an extraordinary person to be the child of an angel and the one man who had sinned. I have, nevertheless, always cherished, in a less literal sense, the thought of my mother as an angel.

It is odd to recall, that, in those early days, my father's story of Satan's mark filled me with anxiety. Often, while I lay on my bed at night after a day in which I might have done something which to my mind was sinful, I passed my hand over my forehead to feel if the mark was there.

Only when I had convinced myself otherwise, could I sleep. And even years later, after I knew that my father's 'brand' had been caused by a piece of flying coal in the mine, I found myself looking at the foreheads of passers-by to see if they carried Satan's mark of sin.

One of the delights of my boyhood was to visit my maternal aunt, and at her house I used to enjoy reading the comic strip in a newspaper. When I asked my father why we didn't have a news-paper at our house I was told: 'It is a thing of the world: there is not enough time to read the Bible.'

At school, *Treasure Island* was one of the set books which I thoroughly enjoyed; but my father told the headmaster that a book about pirates and murder was not fit for children.

But even at that early age, I could not reconcile this argument with the blood and horror of the Old Testament. The answer that the Lord was Jehovah, and, therefore, totally different, I found very unsatisfactory.

The introduction of wireless, and the sight of school friends playing with cat's-whiskers and crystals, prompted the question: 'Why don't we have a wireless set?' My father's answer was that it was an instrument of the devil – a sign of the times – and one day anti-Christ would use the instrument to speak to the world and organize insurrection against God and His Saints. The Brethren were always spoken of as Saints.

The atmosphere of the home was doubtless oppressive for a child. Haigh's parents were devout supporters of the religious movement of which their parents had been among the pioneers, and it was natural that Haigh himself should have been reared in the same tradition and called upon to accept the same beliefs. The Brethren, of whom he speaks and who were described at his trial as 'almost, if not quite, as highly respected a body of persons as the Quakers', provided the religious mould in which Haigh was born, shaped, and made aware.

Early in the nineteenth century certain fervent Christians were appalled by the spectacle of Christendom divided against itself. Seeking an oasis of peace in a distracted world, they strove to prepare for the second coming of Christ by meeting quietly for prayer and meditation. One of the earliest of such communities was formed in Devonshire at Plymouth about 1830. The movement grew in influence and numbers. Historically, its development, along with that of the Broad Church, Evangelical, and Tractarian Movements, was the expression of that craving for some new form of spiritual orientation which characterized early Victorian England.

But the evil of division, with which the Plymouth Brethren, as they came to be called, were so preoccupied, regrettably vitiated their own ranks. It is, therefore, scarcely possible to pen a thumb-nail sketch of the doctrine they all embrace. Generally, it may be said that most of the Brethren adopt an anti-clerical attitude, arrogating to their own assemblies the claim of being the sole representatives of the contemporary Christian Church, the sole rallying point for a divided Christendom.

It was no doubt this element of their teaching which lent substance to the point made in Haigh's defence at his trial that his background of Plymouthism clashed with the ritual of the Cathedral in which he became a chorister.

It is illogical to visit the sins of Haigh upon the tenets of a faith, the sixth Commandment of which is : 'Thou shalt do no murder.' Yet, because religious instruction is so potent a part of education, the influence of Plymouthism upon Haigh's development cannot be wholly disregarded.

At the age of seventeen, before he left school, he delighted his parents by winning a Divinity Prize. The essay on St Peter with which he won the award contained the conclusion: 'We may well learn the lesson that one fall, even though it be met by perfect grace and full restoration, does not cure a natural disposition, though it may go far to correct it.'

So Haigh was already moving towards his fatalistic acceptance of the incurability of a 'natural disposition'. The belief
may have been engendered by the Brethren's Calvinistic
view of the Christian religion and by the doctrine of sancti-
fication by faith, unrelated to works. It is a belief which
becomes a menace when translated into action. Although
the Brethren themselves attain exceptionally high standards
of practical holiness, and it is not here presumed in any way
to censure the body of their doctrines, the two following
brief passages from the authoritative *History and Teaching
of the Plymouth Brethren* by Canon Teulon are peculiarly
pertinent :

If men are taught that if they believe in Christ they will not be
judged at all, or not be judged according to their works, the practical safeguard provided by this great truth is taken away and their
souls become exposed at once to ... forms of temptation ... ; false
principles have a terrible way of working out their natural consequences in those who are nurtured by them.

Again :

When the Brethren tell us not to expect any improvement in our
nature, when they assert that our fallen nature can never be sancti-
fied, they are, unintentionally no doubt, teaching men to acquiesce
in the existence of evils which it should be their lifelong endeavour
to remove.

The canon's criticisms, published in the last century, are
strikingly ominous in the present context.

But, whether the principles on which Haigh was nurtured
were false or true, an immediate consequence of his parents'
somewhat exclusive views was that Haigh himself tended to
live an isolated childhood. Most of the neighbours at Outwood were of a rougher type, and Haigh's quiet, religious
parents did not allow him to mix freely with children of his
own age in the district. He was an only child and a lonely
one. He kept rabbits, and at an early age manifested an
affection for animals. He would give his own food to neighbours' dogs and was sensitive to their maltreatment. It is

said that he was equally generous in giving his toys to the two or three children who were his playmates. Probably his isolation made him introspective and induced him to seek entertainment in his own imagination, even more than do most children.

Apart from solitariness, Haigh's infancy appears to have been normal. His father has stated that he was a good boy: 'Right up to the time he left home he never misbehaved. He had very good health, and there was nothing wrong with him mentally. He got on very well with other boys, but I think he was too generous.' Through all the twists and turns of his life he remained on affectionate terms with his parents.

It is said that as a child he sustained a few minor injuries: at about the age of seven he accidentally and violently struck his ear on the bedroom wardrobe, and a few years later he cut his scalp, when falling downstairs; but on neither occasion was he seen by a doctor.

Haigh afterwards used to assert that his fond mother corrected him during childhood by smacking his hand with the bristles of a hairbrush. When his trial for murder was pending, he added that the punishment of the hairbrush drew blood, which he sucked and enjoyed to such an extent that he later deliberately cut his finger to gratify the taste he had acquired.

The rhythm of his life continued, in spite of the First World War. His home was not disrupted. But, in about 1916, Haigh was taken on holiday to Goole and there witnessed one of the first Zeppelin raids. The experience so upset him that the holiday had to be curtailed; and for several weeks after his return to Outwood, he is said to have remained nervous and depressed.

In the same year, at the age of seven, he was sent to school. After a period at a preparatory school, he attended Wakefield Grammar School until he was seventeen. He still showed no signs of abnormality. But it was noted that as soon as school finished he would return home instead of mingling with his companions. The solitary infant became the solitary schoolboy.

Some of his teachers describe him as having been a mischievous boy; and certain of his other life-long characteristics became apparent at school. He became an inveterate liar; the habit developed as a matter of convenience because, as he put it, the truth often distressed his parents and he preferred to avoid trouble by inventing what he knew they wanted to hear. He was also habitually 'smart' in both senses of the word : quick with his tongue and neat in appearance – a Smart Alec in smart attire. Although he was lazy and made little effort to master subjects which did not capture his imagination, he early developed a scientific bent; and, ever hankering for the limelight, flouted his knowledge. On one occasion he gave a lecture on cotton-spinning, a subject of small appeal to his school-mates. But he failed to pass School Certificate, and measured by examination standards he was an indifferent scholar.

Nor was he an athlete. He loathed the rough and tumble of sports, which, for different reasons, his parents equally disfavoured. Only on compulsory days would he play cricket or football. On the other days he preferred the organ-loft to the playing-fields. Eventually, he managed to procure a medical certificate which excused him from all school games and left him free to indulge his passion for music.

It was music which was the great joy of his life, at school and after. In it he found solace, and an emotional outlet which his childhood's environment otherwise failed to provide. He became an accomplished pianist and acted as organist for minor services in Wakefield Cathedral. In addition, he was chosen, out of the school choir, to join the Cathedral choir. This choral scholarship required him to attend the Cathedral services; but it relieved his parents of the expense they had hitherto borne for his education.

The religious services in which Haigh now participated were highly ritualistic, while the religiosity with which he had grown familiar at home was predominantly puritanical and anti-clerical. From ten to sixteen years of age, he thus lived in two worlds which were superficially, if not fundamentally antithetic. To what extent the dichotomy warped the development of his character is a matter of opinion. At the trial, much emphasis was imposed, on his behalf, on the disturbing and demoralizing consequences which might have ensued from being associated at an impressionable age with two such contrasting religious systems. But it is notable that, at the time, he appeared to welcome the change and relish the voice and verse and colour of High Church ritual. For a while it seems to have given him some sort of emotional vent, and his apparent religious zeal received warm encouragement from home.

Every Sunday was spontaneously spent in religious activities; at 5.30 a.m., Haigh would leave home and walk three miles to officiate as Server at the Cathedral altar for Holy Communion at six, seven, and eight o'clock. He would next attend Matins, Sunday School, and Evensong, ultimately plodding the same three weary miles home again, to prayers with his devout parents.

Later, when his trial was pending, Haigh added that he spent much of the spare time of his school-days in the Cathedral. He said that there, in the fading light, he would sit gazing upon a model of Christ bleeding upon the Cross. 'Why not kill and be done with it and put Him out of His agony?' he thought. At night Christ crucified would appear in Haigh's dreams. In another of his recurring dreams, Haigh built a huge telescopic ladder by which he reached the moon.

After he had described his dreams, someone intimated to him that the colours appearing in them were of interest; and Haigh then added the embellishments that the blood of which he dreamed was red and gory and the globe from his ladder seemed incarnadine.

The importance which Haigh later attached to the motive-power of his dreams was perhaps explained by the interest he had entertained for the subject since he was a boy. He afterwards said that his mother had often bought and studied books on dreams and that he, in turn, had taken the opportunity of reading them. Haigh was known to have inherited his father's propensity for reading and devoured whatever books were available. Nor was it unlikely that his mother was attracted by literature on dreams. Was it not written of Joseph in the Book of Genesis, 'I have heard say of thee, that thou canst understand a dream to interpret it'? Haigh's mother, being steeped in the Scriptures, was no doubt concerned with the details of such dreams as were ascribed to divine agency.

There was, of course, only Haigh's word for what he dreamt and for his assertion, after his final arrest, that since the age of eleven he had been in the habit of drinking his own urine. He did not appear to have developed any morbid sexual traits in early adolescence. He stated that, at the age of twenty, he was introduced by a friend to sex-life, that for a few years he sowed his wild oats, and that he then 'tired' of sex. At the age of twenty-four, he married a beautiful bride, confessedly to escape the restrictions of his parents' home. If freedom was his object, it was scarcely realized; for within a few months of the marriage he was sentenced to imprisonment; and, he said, he never saw his wife again.

Until he married and left his parents' home, Haigh lived an honest life. He took his place in the assembly of the Brethren, where he became an acceptable speaker; and soon after leaving school at the age of seventeen he began to earn a living. Always interested in mechanical work, he was first employed by a firm of motor engineers. After a year he left of his own accord because the work was too dirty; and he took a 'white collar' job instead. From school-days onwards, he was always fastidious about his personal appearance.

At the age of twenty-one, he started a business of his own, said to have been inspired by the famous Hatry case of two years before. He formed a company for advertising, estate agency, and insurance, thereby enabling, for instance, a young doctor to buy an interest in a partnership with the aid of a life assurance. Haigh acted as a sub-broker, working with other brokers. The project promised well. Within a year he was endeavouring to arrange insurance involving £30,000 in connexion with the construction of a dam in Egypt. Within two years, he floated the Northern Electric Newspapers Ltd, another advertising agency which superseded his former venture. Under its auspices a large electrically-lit advertising space was erected in the city square at Leeds.

But Haigh's early triumphs were short-lived. In 1934, the year of rebellion against his upbringing, when he married, left his parents' home, and ceased to attend the meetings of the Brethren, he read in a newspaper of a conviction for selling motor cars obtained on hire-purchase. The crime struck him as an easy means to more money and he explored the idea. In answer to an advertisement, he became the hire-purchase inspector of a company and found the whole system attractively lax. *Facilis descensus Averno*. His greed for gold blinded him to any injury he might do to others, or even to himself.

'When I first discovered there were easier ways to make a living than to work long hours in an office,' he wrote later, 'I did not ask myself whether I was doing right or wrong. That seemed to me to be irrelevant. I merely said : "This is what I wish to do." And as the means lay within my power, that was what I decided.' The passage might have come from the pen of the paranoiacal author of *Mein Kampf*.

So Haigh tried his hand at crime. His device was to advertise for a garage, stating at the same time that the necessary capital was available. From the replies he received, he was careful to select a garage whose owner seemed to be in financial straits. After negotiations, Haigh would take an option to purchase. The owner usually welcomed Haigh's suggestion that, during the option period, the commission on any cars which Haigh sold should be divided between both of them. Haigh, using the address of the garage, would next obtain from a hire-purchase company blank forms of agreement for the hire-purchase of a motor car. Having taught himself at school to imitate the handwriting of others, Haigh was able to complete the forms in the name of some person of standing in the neighbourhood of the garage and return them to the hire-purchase company with particulars of a fictitious purchase by that person of a non-existent car. The company then obligingly advanced the requisite money by a cheque which Haigh himself would endorse and cash. For a few months he escaped detection. On 22 November 1934, however, he was sentenced at Leeds Assizes to fifteen months' (Division 2) imprisonment for conspiring to defraud; aiding and abetting the forgery of a document; and obtaining money by false pretences; with six similar cases taken into consideration.

He seemed genuinely grieved to have dishonoured his parents and wrote to them from prison : 'May God give me time to redeem the past, and to make you happy in your later years.'

While still a prisoner, Haigh received a letter, couched in friendly terms, intimating that his sin had come to the attention of the Brethren. He knew what was meant. The Brethren could not advocate separation from other religious bodies, on the ground that those bodies tolerated evil, and then tolerate evil themselves. He was ostracized from the spiritual cradle into which he had been born. The news came to him, in his own words, 'as somewhat of a shock', and an official of the prison called him aside and expressed the hope that he would not let it get him down. His mother afterwards thought that his expulsion from the community of the Brethren affected his whole attitude to life.

On 8 December 1935, he left prison. The Prodigal Son returned home, forgiven. 'After my release', he wrote, 'I needed work, and successful efforts were made to set me up in a dry-cleaning business, with branches in Leeds, Bradford, and Sheffield. Dry-cleaning is dry-cleaning all the world over, but persuading the public that you can do it better than the rest, or that they will get something better, is quite different. That is an art.'

His earlier experience of the art of advertising must have
stood him in good stead, if there was any truth in his own
success story : 'No other dry-cleaner, I suggest, has opened
a shop and turned over 2,000 garments a week from the
opening. I was thrilled at the success, and had ideas for
improving the general system which would have left the
opposition streets behind. But,' he concluded, 'luck was
against me. My partner was killed in a motor accident in
Ashdown Forest, and his wife did not wish to continue with
any of his ventures. The result was voluntary liquidation to
meet the estate. I was too stunned by this disappointment to
attempt to go on.'

Haigh then went to London. Discovering a vacancy was
advertised for the post of manager of an amusement arcade,
he responded by a telegram which led to an ill-fated introduction. The owner of the business – who employed Haigh
for a short time as a chauffeur and secretary, and found him
'very satisfactory' – was a Mr McSwan of 26 Woodside,
Wimbledon. All three members of the family whom Haigh
met as a result of that advertisement were, in eight or nine
years' time, to be liquidated by him.

Meanwhile, his insatiable lust for money again led him
into temptation. The swindle he next evolved was of the
variety associated with Horatio Bottomley, and may have
been conceived by Haigh when the estate of his partner in
the dry-cleaning business was being wound up.

For the purposes of deception, Haigh opened a spurious
solicitor's office, adopting the name of some reputable firm,
culled from the Law List. Thus disguised, he pretended to
have an estate to wind up and shares for disposal. The shares
were purported to be of a public company with a small
market and were offered at a tempting price, below that at
which they were currently quoted. The invitation to buy
them promised that they would be delivered in due course
to applicants who paid a twenty-five per cent deposit. Within
a couple of days, cheques, representing the deposits, poured
in; and with them Haigh bought all manner of things. As

soon as the cheques were cleared, he collected the goods and the change, absconded from the district, and proceeded elsewhere to gather more ill-gotten gains in a similar way.

Eventually the law overtook him, while operating in Guildford. Mis-spelling was always one of his foibles and it was said to have been his failure to include the middle 'd' in Guildford which contributed to his undoing. On 24 November 1937, at the Surrey Assizes in Kingston, he pleaded guilty to having attempted to obtain £750 by false pretences and to seven cases of obtaining bankers' cheques by false pretences, with twenty-two other similar offences taken into consideration. The total sum involved was £3,172 4s. 8d.

Haigh had been in prison before and had no desire to return to the cells which he regarded as 'inhuman, in-humane, a denial of comfort and hope'. Inwardly, he viewed his fraud with 'great satisfaction'; but he made a dishonest plea from the dock to the effect that he had been misled. 'This type of fraud will continue to be perpetrated after I am sentenced,' he told Mr Justice Charles. 'The man who is responsible is still at large.' Haigh was, nevertheless, sentenced to four years' penal servitude.

So it was that he was still behind bars when war was declared. Not until 13 August 1940 was he released on licence.

He then obtained employment as a firewatcher near St George's Drive in Victoria. Perhaps it was during the current bombing of London that he began to develop his distorted sense of the cheapness of human life. His experiences as a firewatcher 'made one stop and think of the general conception of things,' as he phrased it.

That there was an all-loving God could not very well be reconciled with all that was going on to innocent people.

I loathe suffering. I detest to see humans in pain, or fear, and I was shocked in both mind and spirit. The ghastly sights after two land mines had wiped out a block of buildings are fixed indelibly in my memory.

On one occasion, while on firewatching duty, I was talking to a Red Cross nurse at a warden's post. The sirens shrieked, bombs dropped, and the nurse and I moved off to our places of duty. Suddenly, in a moment of premonition, I knew that a bomb would fall close by. I dodged into a doorway and awaited the inevitable crash. It came with a horrifying shriek, and as I staggered up, bruised and bewildered, a head rolled against my foot.

The nurse who, but a few moments before, had been gay, full of life, high ideals, and sense of duty, had in one instant been swept into eternity. I was shocked beyond all belief. How could God allow it to happen?

As a firewatcher in civil defence, Haigh was in a reserved occupation. Consequently, the formality he in fact performed, in February 1941, of registering for military service was, in effect, a mere gesture. Two years later, when not so employed, and when required to attend before a recruits' medical board, he failed to appear and could not be traced. Eventually, in 1945, his register was marked for no further action.

On 11 June 1941, while still on licence, he was sentenced at County of London Sessions to twenty-one months' hard labour for stealing from a house five bunks with kitchen material worth £15 10s. and for stealing, as a bailee, sixty yards of curtaining and a refrigerator. He bitterly resented being held by the Court to have hired the refrigerator from a café proprietor before selling it. According to his version, he had been asked to sell it by the owner who was dissatisfied with the price obtained. Smarting under what he described as 'a piece of gross injustice', he made up his mind that 'after this, there would be no more *inside* for me'.

But the iron had entered into his soul and his mind was turning to darker thoughts. The ordinary run of criminals he disdained as a bunch of cheap crooks. 'If you are going to go wrong,' he satanically told his fellow-prisoners, 'go wrong in a big way, like me. Go after women – rich, old women who like a bit of flattery. That's your market, if you are after big money.' Another inmate remembered Haigh at Lincoln Prison, employed in the tinsmith's shop, where sulphuric acid was available and in constant use. For a consideration, the prisoners who worked in the fields kept Haigh supplied with field mice on which he would experiment. He is said to have made a special study of the corrosive action of acid on animal tissues. If immersed in its own volume of cold concentrated sulphuric acid, the mouse would decompose. Within ten minutes, the liquid would darken and its temperature gradually rise to 100° Centigrade. In half an hour, it would be nothing but black sludge.

Hitherto, Haigh had been a 'red band' prisoner, a 'shining light in a dark place', as his devoted parents admonished him to be. In Lincoln prison, however, which was in his opinion the worst prison he ever knew, he lost some remission for trafficking in correspondence. Consequently he did not complete his third sentence until 17 September 1943.

For a few weeks he lived with his parents in Leeds. Then, on 25 October, he received a request to attend before a medical board for military service. He ignored it; and, in November, went south again, with the intention of reviving his interest in dry-cleaning. He obtained an introduction to a light-engineering firm in Crawley, however, and for about a year found employment there, obtaining orders and quotations on a commission basis.

Haigh also found that the firm's proprietor, with whom he lived, had a pretty young daughter with a passion for music. Inevitably, the common interest drew them together. The relationship which developed reflected credit on both of them. Out of it she could have made much capital when Haigh was charged with murder: instead, with loyal dignity, she confined her comments to harmless allusions, such as: 'He always spoke with affection of his parents.' Haigh, for his part, reposed in her the implicit trust she merited. When in prison on the capital charge, he wrote to her: 'I know exactly what I may attribute to you in the Press and how much is "parsley round the fish". So please don't worry about that at all.'

Again, in one of the many letters he wrote her from prison

during his last days, recalling 'five happy years', he concluded : 'It is difficult to say farewell under these circumstances, but you will understand that you will be always in my thoughts. You know I have been proud of our association : it has always been an honourable one. I shall remember your great kindness and your devotion. Now I must leave you.'

During the period of his employment at Crawley, Haigh suffered a scalp wound from a motor accident after which, so he said, his school-day dreams recurred. The medical report of his injury reads : '1944. 26 March. 10.15 p.m. Motor Accident. Cut two inches long, left temporal region. Cleansed. 3 Sutures. No foreign body. No sign of alcohol ... 1 April. Stitches out, healed, clear. Nausea morning, reaction.'

Five years later, when in custody, Haigh wrote of the accident :

Blood poured from my head down my face and into my mouth. This revived in me the taste, and that night I experienced another awful dream.

I saw before me a forest of crucifixes, which gradually turned into trees. At first there appeared to be dew, or rain, dripping from the branches, but as I approached I realized it was blood.

Suddenly the whole forest began to writhe and the trees, stark and erect, to ooze blood. ... A man went to each tree catching the blood. ... When the cup was full he approached me. ... 'Drink,' he said, but I was unable to move. The dream faded.

While no one will ever know whether Haigh, with an eye on his defence of insanity, invented the account of his dreams, it is possible that in that same year of 1944 he became haunted by nightmares, like Lady Macbeth, *after* and not before he first began to kill, that the dream was the effect and not the cause of committing murder.

In 1944, Haigh acquired the use of the basement of No. 79 Gloucester Road as a workshop. About the same time, at a public-house in Kensington, he chanced to meet young William Donald McSwan again. Much water had flowed under the bridge since 1936, when Haigh had assisted the McSwans in their ventures. With the advent of war McSwan's amusement arcade had been sold and the proceeds invested in other property. Haigh, for his part, had served two more terms of imprisonment. It was agreeable for both to recover the threads of the past; and, round at No. 45 Claverton Street, the same street in which Edwin Bartlett had died, McSwan's parents were equally delighted to see Haigh again.

Thereafter young 'Mac' and Haigh met frequently. Sometimes they would take supper together and soon Mac confided in Haigh his plan to go underground in order to avoid national service. Haigh, in turn, talked of the girl he had met at Crawley who was fond of music and skilled at shorthand. Mac also had mastered shorthand. Haigh had not. So one evening, Mac wrote in shorthand, at Haigh's dictation, the following postcard :

Barbara Darling,

Thanks a million for your postcard which was a very pleasant surprise. I had actually had a distinctly harassing day today, that is Tuesday, and therefore your card had an added attraction. It was very sweet of you to think of sending it and you don't know – or perhaps you do – how much I appreciate the kindly thought which sponsored it. I have no doubt that actually it was a cunning piece of work calculated to inveigle me into writing the first letter. You are a naughty little girl and it does not work. However, you are such a good little girl for having sent it at all that I will overcome that little bit of intrigue. I am awfully glad you did not come to the station with me on Saturday because the train was desperately late. I felt frightfully lonely on Sunday and went up to see Doreen and Gordon. Doreen said, 'What on earth's the matter with you, Haigh? You look thoroughly fed up.' So I explained I was feeling a little lonely and left it at that. She's by the way looking forward to seeing you when you come up to town which I should imagine should not be far off as you can take it for granted that the buzz-bombs (doodles) are a thing of the past. I hope you find this bit of Mr Pitman's amusing and I hope you will be able to read it because otherwise you will have to take it along to Cossy since I cannot, as you know. I have been giving Mac a hand tonight out at Elstree and as I never work for nothing my charge is this bit of stenography. It serves a dual purpose. It should keep you amused for a couple of hours and of course the Nipper will not be able to read it. The weather has been appalling since you left but I hope you are enjoying yourself although not to the extent of wanting to make a fortnight of it because I am anxiously looking forward to your return. If you return this weekend I shall pop over on Monday or Tuesday so please be good enough to let me know.

All my love darling, Yours ever,

(Signed) John

John's let my cocoa get cold – Mac.

The postmark is dated 6 September 1944.

Then suddenly Mac disappeared, and has never been seen since. Subsequently, the sign of the cross, inscribed in red crayon, was discovered in Haigh's diary, under 9 September 1944. The cryptic entry has been explained by Haigh in the following terms :

I got the feeling I must get some blood somewhere. I was quite capable of carrying on business in an abstract sort of way. I was meeting McSwan from time to time. . . . He brought a pin-table to Gloucester Road to repair. The idea then came to me to kill him and take some blood. I hit him over the head and he was unconscious. I got a mug and took some blood, from his neck, in the mug, and drank it. Then I realized I must do something about him. I left him there dead. That night I had the dream when I caught up with the blood. At Gloucester Road I had acid and sheet metal for pickling. I found a water butt on a disused site and took it on a cart and put McSwan in acid. I put the body in the tub and poured the acid on it. I did it with a bucket. I went to see McSwan's parents and told them he had gone away because of his call-up. I sent them a letter from Glasgow.

On 12 September Haigh happened to mention in a personal letter from London that he was suffering from enteritis. Possibly the complaint was caused by drinking the blood of W. D. McSwan. On the other hand, Haigh's positive statement that he was never sick after his blood-drinking casts doubt on whether he ever indulged in the habit, because human blood, drunk neat, is almost bound to act as an emetic. But whether or not he drank his victim's blood, there is little doubt that, on 9 September 1944, Haigh killed William Donald McSwan at 79 Gloucester Road. It was probably the first murder he committed.

About two months or more later, according to Haigh's statement to the police, he murdered in similar circumstances a middle-aged woman, who cannot be identified from the slender information he has given of her. No evidence other than Haigh's word is available to substantiate his assertion and one wonders whether the account of the incident, contained in his statement, is true.

But, again, there is little doubt that he murdered both parents of W. D. McSwan, as he said he did. No trace of the existence of either of them after 2 July 1945 can be found. Haigh incorrectly gave the police the date of this double murder as 1946 : it probably occurred during the first week of July 1945.

As to the motive of the murder, Haigh said it was because the father's corpse did not produce enough blood that he killed the mother on the same day. On the other hand, Haigh could not have expected to bring within his grasp the Mc-Swans' property so long as a member of that family were alive. After having exterminated the whole family of three, he proceeded to appropriate their estates.

By 16 July he was in Carlisle, scribbling, in a letter, with characteristic composure : 'To the Southerner, Northern scenery is hard and forbidding : but to me there is a homely frankness about the bleak moors ribboned with stone walls.'

Two days later, in Glasgow, he fraudulently obtained control of his victim's assets. Pretending to be young W. D. Mc-Swan, Haigh entered a solicitor's office and in the presence of witnesses forged McSwan's signature on a Power of Attorney. The instrument gave Haigh power to deal with McSwan's possessions and specified four freehold properties:

9 Grand Drive, Raynes Park; 104 Kenilworth Avenue, Wimbledon Park; 15 Wimborne Way, Beckenham; and 112 Churchfields Road, Beckenham. Although the first three premises belonged to W. D. McSwan, the fourth was in fact owned by McSwan's murdered mother. Haigh consequently forged a deed, dated 9 October 1945, purporting to convey this property from the mother to the son, in consideration of £500.

Having instructed solicitors in London to enrol the forged Power of Attorney in the Central Office of the Supreme Court, Haigh dealt with all the properties named in it. The series of transactions which followed was involved and prolonged. They appear from Haigh's files to have enriched him to the extent of about £1,720 net.

In addition, Haigh is known to have obtained, by means of forged transfers, £2,107 worth of gilt-edged securities held by the McSwan family, and to have profited from the sale of their furniture, household effects, and personal belongings. It may be assumed that he gained £4,000 from the possessions of that family alone. Their disappearance was never reported to the police, and went unnoticed until Haigh divulged the secret at the Chelsea Police Station on 28 February 1949.

Meanwhile, by 1945, Haigh had left Crawley and come to live in South Kensington, at Onslow Court Hotel. With the object of acting as liaison officer between patentees, inventors, and engineering firms, he began to use the name of Union Group Engineering. He went to the trouble of obtaining specially printed stationery, which described the concern as having branches in Crawley, Croydon, Putney, and Wimbledon. In fact, the only known address of the business was the Onslow Court Hotel, where Haigh occupied one furnished room. He submitted no income-tax returns and his income from his engineering activities has not been ascertained. But it is known that in 1945 one inventor agreed to allot a fifty per cent interest in all his inventions to Haigh, in consideration of capital supplied and services rendered by

Haigh. It was to exploit these inventions that Haigh paid
the £225 mentioned by Mr Jones in his evidence. The inventor himself died in March 1948, and it remained one of
Haigh's constant prepossessions to develop the by no means
worthless patents in which he and the deceased inventor had
been mutually interested. Even when under sentence of
death, Haigh wrote several letters about the legal position
of the patents and the welfare of the inventor's widow and
children, whom he affectionately described as 'the most wonderful family that any man could be privileged to know'.

In the autumn of 1945, Haigh, so he said, killed a youth
named Max, at 79 Gloucester Road. But, as in his claim to
have killed a woman in the preceding February, so in this
case he failed to supply the police with information which
would enable them to test the truth of his statement.

The probabilities are that, by the end of 1945, despite his
claim to five victims, Haigh had murdered no one other than
the three McSwans and, like a vulture engorging their
corpses, was helping himself to their property. At Christmas,
he was pleased with his progress and wrote in high spirits
that he would love to send the compliments of the season to
all the old ladies at the Onslow Court Hotel and to those
dear old gentlemen who doled him out a paltry forty units
of petrol. 'In fact,' he elatedly continued, 'a right merry
Christmas I say to all taxi-drivers, muffin men, window
cleaners, chestnut vendors, laundry men, watch repairers
and, last but not least, to those unseen friends, brewers'
draymen. Oh, and finally : joy to Austerity's Sweetheart,
Sir Stafford Cripps, who, so far as I can gather, never lightly
discards anything – even an acid drop. . . . You see I'm feeling quite content with the world.'

Perhaps Haigh's banking account supplies the reason for
his contentment. In 1944, £347 were paid in, in 1945,
£1,211, and in the following two years a total of no less than
£5,655.

Yet, by the beginning of August 1947, the account showed
a debit balance of £25 5s. 2d. The murdering of the Mc-

Swans had brought Haigh a windfall. But he had spent it all and more. Running again into financial difficulties, he was, no doubt, watching for some other likely prey. Eleven years ago, it was by answering an advertisement that he had first met the McSwans; now, in September 1947, it was by answering an advertisement that he met Dr and Mrs Henderson.

The Hendersons' house at 22 Ladbroke Square, w 11, was for sale and the advertisement of the sale caught Haigh's eye. Despite his debts he entered into negotiations, offering considerably more for the house than was asked. When it came to the point, he could not find the money and the deal was not completed. But Haigh had met the Hendersons and he spent the next four or five months cultivating their friendship. He was so kind, thought Mrs Henderson, and could not do enough for her and the Doctor. Haigh, for his part, deceitful and treacherous as ever, had no intention of respecting the trust which he was so assiduously fostering. His dealings with the Hendersons conformed to the same nauseating patterns of conduct as that which characterized his treatment of the McSwans, and, later of Mrs Durand-Deacon.

On at least two occasions in December 1947, Haigh took possession of the keys of that storehouse which he used for 'experimental purposes' in Crawley. On 22 December, he ordered himself a Christmas present of three carboys of sulphuric acid, from the same firm as that from which he obtained acid a year later when Mrs Durand-Deacon disappeared. Similarly, in both cases he asked the same engineer in Crawley to bring the acid from London to Crawley. On 29 December 1947, Haigh was careful to pay £4 8s. 7d. for the acid, although he was by no means solvent at the time. Early in February 1948, Mr Jones of Crawley noticed two or three carboys of acid in the storehouse. About the same time, Haigh ordered two forty-gallon drums, the tops of which were, in accordance with his instructions, to be removed. Thus was the stage set in the storehouse for one of Haigh's terrible 'experiments'.

His next concern was to entice the Hendersons to the death chamber. They had sold their house in Ladbroke Square and bought 16 Dawes Road, Fulham. On 7 February 1948, they left London in unaccountable haste and spent three days at Broadstairs, where Haigh visited them. On 10 February, he accompanied them from there to Brighton, where the Hendersons spent the next two nights at the Hotel Metropole. Their red setter dog, Pat, was with them.

'During this period,' said Haigh, 'my dream cycle had commenced.' Coincidentally, it was during this period that his debts had mounted. On 12 February, his overdraft at the bank stood at £237 0s. 11d., his bill at the Onslow Court Hotel required payment, and he also owed a financier £400. But no reference to his financial predicament is contained in his own description of what happened that morning :

... by now I was seized with an awful urge. Once more I saw the forest of crucifixes which changed to trees dripping with blood. Once more I wakened with the desire which demanded fulfilment.

Archie was to be the next victim. I drove him to Crawley, and in the store-room at Leopold Road I shot him in the head with his own revolver, which I had taken from Dawes Road.

I then returned to Brighton, and told Rose that Archie had been taken ill very suddenly and needed her. I said I would drive her to him. She accompanied me to the store-room at Crawley, and there I shot her. From each of them I took my draught of blood.

No one has been found who has seen Dr Archibald Henderson or his wife, Rosalie, or received a genuine communication from either of them, since 12 February 1948. In relation to that date, Haigh's diary, found among his papers, contained two laconic epitaphs : an 'A.H.' for Archibald, and an 'R.H.' for Rosalie Henderson, followed by the sign of the cross.

It was in the early hours of, probably, the following morning that the night porter at the Hotel Metropole, Brighton, was requested by a person, who gave the name of 'Mrs Henderson', to take her red setter out and look after him until the caller returned to the hotel the following day. The ordinary speaking voice of Haigh was always peculiarly highly pitched.

On the 16th, Haigh went to the Brighton hotel where the Hendersons had been staying. He paid their bill and, having produced a letter of authority purporting to be signed by Dr Henderson, Haigh arranged for the Hendersons' luggage to be packed, took the red setter for a walk, and then drove away in his car with the dog, three suit-cases, one soft hold-all, four coats, and two golf-bags, all of which had belonged to the Hendersons.

Besides dissolving the Hendersons' mortal remains in sulphuric acid, Haigh was busy disposing of their property for ready cash. Already, on 15 February, his bank account had been credited with £505. On the 17th, when he paid the Onslow Court Hotel £30, a further cheque was credited to his bank account for £200 from Messrs Bull of Horsham. To them Haigh had sold some jewellery which may now be presumed to have belonged to the Hendersons. It was at the same shop that he subsequently sold the jewellery of Mrs Durand-Deacon. On 11 March 1948, another cheque for £10 was credited to his account from, surprisingly enough, Mrs Durand-Deacon; Haigh had sold her a high-quality handbag, which also presumably belonged to Mrs Henderson.

Nor did Haigh stop there; he sold Dr Henderson's motor car for £400, and, by forged deeds, as in the case of the McSwans, he acquired and sold the Hendersons' house at 16 Dawes Road. Two credit entries in his banking account for June and July 1948, amounting to a total of £2,220 17s. 11d., relate to the transaction. Among the papers subsequently found in Haigh's possession were documents showing that Dr Henderson was the owner of 16 Dawes Road and that Haigh sold the property in July 1948. The total sum of payments into Haigh's account during the year is said to have been £7,771.

Haigh stated in prison that he had had no reason to anticipate financial gain from Dr and Mrs Henderson. He alleged that it was simply a thirst for blood, stimulated by dreams, which impelled him to kill, and that he believed himself to be under some form of divine protection.

'Again,' he callously wrote of his killing of the Hendersons, 'I felt convinced there was an overseeing hand which would protect me. This, and not carelessness, explains why I left Archie in the store-room while I went for (*a*) gas-mask and (*b*) a drum, during the Friday afternoon, and why I left him and Rose (both trussed turkeywise) whilst I got another tank for her on the Saturday. And, also why, on seeing his foot almost complete on emptying the sludge, I left it without troubling to reduce it.'

A year later Haigh's private opinion was that it was Dr Henderson's foot which was found in the sludge at Crawley, and which was said by the experts to be that of Mrs Durand-Deacon. But, either way, it was a point of no very great importance.

'My next task,' Haigh continued, 'was to satisfy everyone who inquired about the Hendersons, and I did this by writing to her housekeeper and brother, copying Rose's handwriting and signature. I explained that difficulties had suddenly arisen, and that they decided to emigrate to South Africa.'

The letters Haigh wrote, as from Mrs Henderson, were masterpieces of forgery. But her unfortunate only brother, Mr Arnold Henry Burlin, was naturally worried, and the forged letters only served to silence him temporarily. On Haigh's mental list of people who might well be liquidated, Mr Burlin must have occupied a place of priority. If alive, Mr Burlin was sure, sooner or later, to inform the police of the disappearance of his sister and her husband. At 6 p.m. on the very day when Haigh sold Mrs Durand-Deacon's jewellery in Horsham, Mr Burlin caused a message to be broadcast by the BBC, requesting Mrs Henderson to visit her mother, who was in fact dangerously ill. Mr Burlin was indeed hot on the trail and Haigh knew it.

It happened that the first information the police received of the disappearance of Dr and Mrs Henderson was Haigh's own statement on 28 February 1949. Haigh must have appreciated by then that any attempt to continue concealing his dual murder of the Hendersons would be pointless; it was, in the circumstances, obvious that the police, even without Haigh's assistance, would have discovered it.

The sad story of the Hendersons ended on 18 January 1950, in the Probate, Divorce, and Admiralty Division of the High Court, when Mr Justice Willmer gave leave to Dr Henderson's sister to swear that her brother died on or since 12 February 1948. She was granted letters of administration of the estate. J. E. S. Simon appeared for the applicant. Haigh's diary was produced in evidence and his confession was exhibited to an affidavit sworn by Chief Inspector Symes, while other corroborative evidence was given on affidavit. The judge concluded that Dr Henderson could be presumed to be dead and an order was made accordingly.

Although Haigh undoubtedly killed Dr and Mrs Henderson as he said, his statement that he next killed a girl named Mary from Eastbourne in the autumn of the same year was not necessarily true. She belonged to the same category as the woman from Hammersmith and the youth from Kensington, whom he claimed to have killed but who may never have existed.

The loss of Haigh's Lagonda car in June 1948 was another mystery. He had been heard to say that he was tired of the 'old rattle-trap' and that he wished someone would steal it. Shortly afterwards it was reported to have been stolen, and was found at the foot of Beachy Head, evidently having crashed over an inaccessible part of the cliff. 'Poor little motor,' wrote Haigh on 29 June 1948, 'it looked awfully sorry for itself and I'm afraid it's a complete write-off. Now we must look for another.' An unidentified body was, at the same time, found near by. 'Some silly wench had followed the car down', as Haigh put it. Even after his arrest, Haigh was most anxious to exculpate himself of all blame for the incident.

Since 1945, he possessed a number of cars all of which, except for that of Dr Henderson, were apparently obtained by hire-purchase. Haigh's transactions in relation to his last car, an Alvis, were typical of his sinuous methods.

He obtained the car by hire-purchase through a finance company, to whom he was consequently in debt to the tune of £188. Nevertheless, in October 1948, he sold the car for £250 to someone, from whom he arranged to hire it back at £5 a week, which he never paid. Then in January 1949, Haigh deposited the log-book with someone else, from whom he obtained a loan of £300 against security of the same car and from whom he arranged to hire it at £10 a month. By February 1949, his debts under these transactions alone amounted to over £500.

By the end of 1948, he had dissipated the substantial sums of money he had obtained. Much of it was squandered in gambling, and he owed five firms of commission agents a total amount of £352 15s. 8d. He also had a bank overdraft of £83 5s. 10d. In addition, so long as he continued to live at the Onslow Court Hotel, he owed the management £5 15s. 6d. a week and a ten per cent charge for services.

Again in debt, he was once more on the prowl for a promising victim. His financial embarrassment was acute and he had no time to spare. A seemingly wealthy widow occupied the table next to his in the dining-room of his hotel, and he snatched at the first opportunity of inducing her to accompany him to the storehouse at Crawley. Within four days of murdering Mrs Durand-Deacon, he realized £110 on her belongings and would certainly have made a further profit of about £50 on the sale of her Persian lamb coat, had he not been arrested.

*

In retrospect, the first twenty years of Haigh's life were in marked contrast to the last twenty. Set against the bright promise of his youth, the dark deeds of the grown man present a chiaroscuro effect. The first half of his life was as impeccable as the second half was demonic and damnable. When the temptation of enrichment by dishonest means suggested itself to him, at the age of twenty-four his weak moral fibre snapped, and the rest of his life was stained with crime, the curve of which steadily steepened. Though he liked to regard his achievements as a work of art, they amounted to one prolonged fraud, in the wake of which were strewn the bodies of six innocent victims.

True, he claimed to have killed nine persons. But of three of them nothing has been discovered to confirm the little he seemed able to say about them when he was in prison. The confession of anyone under arrest on a capital charge must be scrutinized with caution. When made by a liar like Haigh, it is doubly suspect. That he had killed three casual acquaintances was stated by Haigh four days after he had admitted having killed the three McSwans, the two Hendersons, and Mrs Durand-Deacon. It was added after he had taken care to satisfy himself that the police were convinced he had committed those six murders. Haigh knew how much he had pocketed as a result of the six murders; and he had time to reflect on the fatal effect which evidence of his gains would have upon his defence of insanity. There was, therefore, an obvious motive for him to fabricate a story about having killed three anonymous creatures, about whom no evidence could be brought to show he had gained a farthing from the slaughter. The information he gave of each of the three was insufficient for the purpose of identifying any of them. It is worth noting, in passing, the personal factor that the statement about them was made to Inspector Webb, and that Haigh selected the same police officer in whom to confide about the chances of getting out of Broadmoor. Though not impossible, it is, in all the circumstances, highly improbable that Haigh ever killed anyone but the three McSwans, the two Hendersons, and Mrs Durand-Deacon. When he arrived at Lewes Prison on 2 March 1949, he was heard to comment to the Reception Officer : 'This is the result of doing six people, but not for personal gain.'

'It was not their money but their blood that I was after,' Haigh claimed in relation to all his victims.

The thing I am really conscious of is the cup of blood which is constantly before me.

I shot some of my victims, but I couldn't say if I shot them in the head, if the hole was not there to show afterwards. But I can say I made a small cut, usually in the right side of the neck, and drank the blood for three to five minutes, and that afterwards I felt better. Before each of the killings I have detailed in my confession, I had my series of dreams, and another common factor was that the dream cycle started early in the week, and culminated on a Friday.

Apart from his own unreliable word and a bloodstained pen-knife found in his car, there is no indication that Haigh was a psycopathic vampire. It should be remembered that for four and half years he had been a murderer at large. Newspaper reports of murder trials during that period must have held for him an intense personal interest. For instance, he followed closely the trial of Neville George Heath, in which the defence was one of insanity. Haigh had, therefore, ample time to evolve his own version of such a defence.

He was well aware that humans have been known to drink blood since primeval times. The phenomenon has not been confined to the symbolism of religious ritual. It has occurred in history in other connexions. About 300 B.C. there is an account in the *Mahavagga* of a certain Buddhist monk who suffered from a seemingly incurable disease. He went to a place where swine were slaughtered, ate their raw flesh and drank their blood, and his sickness abated.

Again, primitive head-hunters and warriors have been known to believe that the blood of their victims, if drunk, will engender bravery; and, even during the Second World War, it was not unknown for colonial troops stationed in Europe to visit local abattoirs and to drink the fresh blood of sheep and bullocks for the same reason. A yet more recent throwback of a similar tradition appears in Kenya to have induced the Mau Mau initiates to lick the blood of newly slain goats.

Further, some primitive tribes have, from time immemorial, cherished the belief that by tasting the blood of a slain person the slayer will enjoy such a fusion of blood in his veins as to form a communion of friendship with his victim and avert the evils of an avenging spirit. But, in such cases, the killer is usually prompted only to lick the blood, for instance from the lethal weapon, and not to drink it as Haigh claimed he had done.

In all these instances, moreover, the drinking of blood is actuated by a belief in its salutary effect and not associated in any way with psychopathic behaviour. In the very rare case of a spontaneous impulse to drink human blood, the desire has invariably been connected with a sexual perversion. Even then, it has been only incidental, in the frenzy of sexual excitement. In Haigh's life, on the other hand, there is nothing to suggest sexual abnormality.

It is probable that he acquired his knowledge of blood-drinking from the literature he had read on the subject, and that he exploited the idea in an attempt to substantiate his plea of insanity and to escape execution – 'not a bad idea', as he is said to have cockily described it, after his trial was over.

The thoroughness with which the mental condition of a prisoner is considered before he is executed was illustrated by the fact that Haigh's mental condition was carefully examined in prison by no fewer than twelve medical doctors. He was given various tests, including one by electro-encephalogram, an instrument which records the currents arising within the head from activity in the nerve centres. The result of that test was essentially normal. Between his arrest and trial Haigh was examined, separately, for many hours at different periods, by four experienced prison medical officers, all of whom were satisfied that he was responsible for his actions and merely malingering insanity.

In addition, he was examined for the defence by three eminent consulting London psychiatrists, none of whom was able to say that Haigh was not responsible for his actions. One of them, Dr Yellowlees, gave evidence at the trial; he believed Haigh to be mentally ill and abnormal but responsible.

'Dear Sir,' wrote Haigh to him from the condemned cell, 'I would like you to know that I appreciate the personal interest you have taken and the effort you have made on my behalf even though I cannot agree with your opinion. After all, all the outstanding personalities throughout history have been considered odd : Confucius, Jesus Christ, Julius Caesar, Mahomet, Napoleon, and even Hitler; all possessed a greater perception of the infinite and a more lucid understanding of the omniscient mind. I am happy to inform you that my mother, writing to me during last week, was able to confirm that my headmistress at the High School and my headmaster at the Grammar School both reported that I was not at all a normal boy. How could it be otherwise in the product of an angel and one of the few men who ever sinned?

'I do therefore have the utmost admiration for your greater perception and am grateful for your courageous exposition of it. Yours truly, J. G. Haigh.'

After conviction, Haigh was transferred to Wandsworth Prison, where he came under the daily observation of two other medical officers, neither of whom had reason to think he was insane.

Finally, the Home Secretary carefully considered the circumstances of the case and caused a special medical inquiry to be made as to Haigh's mental condition, under Section 2 (4) of the Criminal Lunatics Act, 1884. It was an extensive inquiry; and all three psychiatrists appointed to hold it were agreed that Haigh was simulating insanity and that there was not the slightest reason to believe he was irresponsible according to legal standards, or insane according to medical standards. It was, therefore, not surprising that the Secretary of State was unable to find any sufficient ground to justify him in advising His Majesty to interfere with the course of the law.

John George Haigh was executed at Wandsworth Prison on 6 August 1949.

Discover more about our forthcoming books through Penguin's FREE newspaper...

Penguin
Quarterly

It's packed with:

- exciting features
- author interviews
- previews & reviews
- books from your favourite films & TV series
- exclusive competitions & much, much more...

Write off for your free copy today to:
Dept JC
Penguin Books Ltd
FREEPOST
West Drayton
Middlesex
UB7 0BR
NO STAMP REQUIRED

READ MORE IN PENGUIN

READ MORE IN PENGUIN

A SELECTION OF CRIME AND MYSTERY

Devices and Desires P. D. James

When Commander Adam Dalgliesh becomes involved in the hunt for the killer in a remote area of the Norfolk coast, he finds himself caught up in the dangerous secrets of the headland community. And then one moonlit night it becomes chillingly apparent that there is more than one killer at work in Larsoken…

Blood Rights Mike Phillips

Being black didn't actually qualify journalist Sam Dean for locating people – even in Notting Hill. But for the Tory MP with the missing teenage daughter it was enough. And then Sam was known for his discretion. His overdraft and his curiosity outweighing his misgivings, Sam agrees to turn private eye. His journey through London's twilight world exposes a drama of political scandal and racial tension.

Death's Bright Angel Janet Neel

At Britex Fabrics Francesca Wilson's economic investigation and John McLeish's murder inquiry are getting inextricably confused – with an American senator, a pop star and the Bach Choir as well as each other… 'Sharp, intelligent and amusing' – *Independent*

Rough Treatment John Harvey

When Grabianski and Grice break into the TV director's house they don't expect to find his wife nursing a glass of Scotch and several years of frustration – or a kilo of cocaine in the safe. As Detective Inspector Charlie Resnick goes after them, he discovers a criss-cross of deceit and greed, adultery and corruption.

The Big Sleep Raymond Chandler

Millionaire General Sternwood, a paralysed old man, is already two-thirds dead. He has two beautiful daughters – one a gambler, the other a degenerate – and an elusive adventurer as a son-in-law. The General is being blackmailed, and Marlowe's assignment is to get the blackmailer off his back. As it turns out, there's a lot more at stake…

READ MORE IN PENGUIN

A SELECTION OF CRIME AND MYSTERY

Stardust Robert B. Parker

Why would anyone want to harm America's sweetheart? That's what Spenser has been hired to find out. But he may have signed on for more than he's bargained, as his client is the glamorous TV star Jill Joyce. A spoilt brat with a murky past, she may be her own worst enemy. But Spenser's not taking any chances. Her life may be in serious danger, and, as the cool, fast-talking detective knows, there's no curtain call for homicide.

Death and the Maiden Sheila Radley

The girl had drowned in a shallow brook, surrounded by wild flowers. It was the first Chief Inspector Quantrill, working in the small East Anglian district of Ashthorpe and Beckenham Market, had heard of Ophelia... 'Here is an author who can be bracketed with the best' – *Observer*

Birth Marks Sarah Dunant

'Make way for Hannah Wolfe, one of the best private eyes, either sex, either side of the Atlantic' – *Daily Telegraph*. 'Dunant's barbed observations of life and men and things that go wrong are a delight. Intelligent, extremely well written and compassionate' – *The Times*

Deadlock Sara Paretsky

Vic Warshawski is a woman to be reckoned with – a professional detective with a personal interest in her current case. Ex-ice hockey champ Boom Boom was Vic's cousin. But now he's dead, and Vic suspects that his fall over the side of a wharf was murder...

The Pale Criminal Philip Kerr

A brutal murderer on the streets isn't unusual for Berlin in 1938. But this one's killing young Aryan girls, and the Jew who's framed proves innocent. Embarrassing. And Obergruppenführer Heydrich doesn't want a pogrom. So – a little blackmail, and private eye Bernie Gunther finds himself on the trail of the real killer, pursuing some very high-powered suspects through the crankiest sub-cultures of Nazism...

READ MORE IN PENGUIN

A SELECTION OF CRIME AND MYSTERY

The Blunderer Patricia Highsmith

Walter Stackhouse wishes his wife was dead. His wish comes true when Clara's body is found at the bottom of a cliff. But there are uncanny similarities between her death and that of a woman called Helen Kimmel – murdered by her husband… 'Almost unputdownable' – *Observer*

Death of a Partner Janet Neel

His relationship with wilful girlfriend Francesca on the rocks, a harassed Detective Chief Inspector John McLeish is assigned to the case of missing Angela Morgan. An attractive, wealthy lobbyist, and fiancée to a high-ranking government minister, Angela courted success – and the envy of her detractors. When her badly decomposed body is found a week later, the shock waves ripple through Whitehall, and only the murderer knows why.

Maigret and the Madwoman Georges Simenon

Maigret's underlings called her the Madwoman. Yet in fact she was a respectable widow who was convinced that someone followed her when she spent the afternoons in the park. The old lady claimed that it was a matter of life and death; she demanded an interview with her hero, Chief Superintendent Maigret. He agreed. But before he can do so, she is murdered.

The Thirty-Nine Steps John Buchan

In this gripping tale of the hunt for a wanted man – the innocent Richard Hannay – John Buchan created one of the most famous and admired thrillers of all time. With the creation of Richard Hannay, a South African mining engineer and war hero, John Buchan established himself as one of Britain's finest writers of suspense stories.

Vanishing Ladies Ed McBain

A peaceful lake, a cabin in the country, and each other… It looked as though it was going to be an idyllic holiday for Phil Colby and his fiancée Anne. But then Anne disappears from her motel room, and Phil finds a red-haired hooker in her place…

READ MORE IN PENGUIN

A SELECTION OF CLASSIC CRIME

The Daughter of Time Josephine Tey

Now established as one of the most popular and enduring of crime classics, *The Daughter of Time* investigates the questions that surround Richard III, the most hated King of England. Both detective story and enthralling mystery, *The Daughter of Time* is one of the most original pieces of historical fiction ever written.

Death under Sail C. P. Snow

Six guests are detained on their murdered host's wherry halfway through a holiday on the Norfolk Broads. One of them has killed Roger Mills, and, as the enigmatic Finbow points out, all of them hated him... 'Stimulating and satisfying' – *The Times Literary Supplement*

Fen Country Edmund Crispin

Gervase Fen, Oxford don, vain and eccentric amateur detective, together with the self-effacing Detective Inspector Humbleby, solve some of the most bizarre cases in the annals of crime.

The Thin Man Dashiell Hammett

All it took was a little persuasion. Like four .32 bullets, a blonde, the newspapers, the cops and a junked-up hoodlum in his bedroom. Nick Charles, retired Trans-American Detective Agency Ace, was back in business!

Police at the Funeral Margery Allingham

Great Aunt Caroline rules the roost in an old Cambridge residence which is riddled with mystery, evil ... and terror. Uncle Andrew is dead, Aunt Julia is poisoned, Uncle William attacked ... and once again Albert Campion comes to the rescue. With her customary skill Margery Allingham takes the reader through a delightful maze of intrigue.

READ MORE IN PENGUIN

A SELECTION OF CLASSIC CRIME

Wall of Eyes Margaret Millar

Kelsey has become bitter since the accident that left her blind. She was driving the car that night. Geraldine did die, and Kelsey will never see again. But that was two long years ago. Time enough to heal. So why would Kelsey now want to end her life with a grain of morphine? 'She is in the very top rank of crime writers' – Julian Symons

Sweet Danger Margery Allingham

'That was the beauty of Campion; one never knew where he was going to turn up next – at the Third Levée or swinging from a chandelier...' Sweet Danger is perfectly crafted, full of surprising twists and turns. What starts as a light-hearted, slightly crazy wild-goose chase becomes something much more dangerous, nasty and sinister.

Appleby's Other Story Michael Innes

The Chief Constable takes Sir John Appleby to call on a neighbouring stately home. But the owner, Maurice Tytherton, is unable to receive his visitors. He has just been killed. And Appleby, though now retired, cannot overcome his policeman's instincts...

The Franchise Affair Josephine Tey

The Franchise is the name of a large country house in which Marion Sharpe and her mother live. The Affair concerns the accusation by a fifteen-year-old schoolgirl that these two apparently respectable ladies kept her locked up in their attic for a month, beat her, and starved her.